Viewdata revolution

Viewdata revolution

Sam Fedida
Rex Malik

A HALSTED PRESS BOOK

JOHN WILEY & SONS
New York — Toronto

All Rights Reserved. No part of this publication may be reproduced, stored in a retrieval system or transmitted in any form or by any means: electronic, electrostatic, magnetic tape, mechanical, photocopying or otherwise, without permission in writing from the publishers

English language edition, except USA and Canada published by
Associated Business Press, an imprint of
Associated Business Programmes Ltd
Ludgate House
107-111 Fleet Street
London EC4A 2AB

Published in USA and Canada by
Halsted Press, a division of John Wiley & Sons Inc
New York

First published 1979

Library of Congress Cataloguing in Publication Data

Fedida, Sam
   Viewdata revolution

   "A Halsted Press book."

   Includes index.

   1. Data transmission systems. 2. Information storage and retrieval systems. 3. Television systems.
I. Malik, Rex, 1928- joint author. II. Title.
TK5105.F44   1979   384.6'4   79-23869
ISBN 0-470-26879-4

© copyright S. Fedida and R. Malik 1979

Typeset by Photo-Graphics, Honiton, Devon.
Printed and bound in Great Britain by
Redwood Burn Ltd., Trowbridge & Esher

Contents

1	Introduction	1
2	Information retrieval	32
3	Electronic mail	49
4	Electronic funds transfer	81
5	Education	93
6	Viewdata as calculator	103
7	Viewdata games	107
8	The electronic diary	113
9	Viewdata systems	116
10	The future: section one	129
11	The future: section two	144
12	Conclusion	162
Appendix: And now, Videotex		170
Index		184

1 Introduction

'A new medium is never an addition to an old one, nor does it leave the old one in peace. It never ceases to oppress the older media until it finds new shapes and positions for them.'
Understanding Media, 1974

It is doubtful if hubris could be carried further. We believe that Viewdata is a major new medium according to the McLuhan definition; one comparable with print, radio, and television, and which could have as significant effects on society and our lives as those did and still do. Like them, it may well lead to major changes in social habits and styles of life, and have long-lasting as well as complex economic effects.

Viewdata, in our view, is as critical to the development of the 'third' industrial revolution as were the steam engine to the first and the internal combustion engine to the second. It will be one of the key systems of the 'silicon revolution', which in turn is one of the cornerstones of 'The Information Society'.

Why then hubris? Because Viewdata is the invention of one of the authors, Sam Fedida, brought to fruition by him when working as Manager, Computer Applications, in the Research Establishment of the British Post Office. However, this is not self-seeking advertisement, even though the claims we make for

Viewdata may at first sight seem extravagantly large. We make the claims because Viewdata is the first of the systems to enable the mass market to be offered the wide range of services inherent in the mix of computing and telecommunications; the first to bring the power of this combination directly to the general public at prices they seem likely to pay, prices substantially below those involved in computing as we have hitherto understood it.

This has been a major aim — a dream if you will — implicit in computing since the beginning.

What is Viewdata?

So what is Viewdata? It is the name given to a branch of technology (which includes a system known as Teletext, see page 8) initially being brought to the market by the British Post Office under the trade name Prestel. Prestel can be considered the UK version of Viewdata technology's Model-T Ford, but this does not exclude possible Volkswagens, Peugeots, Chryslers and the rest. Nor, further up market, does it exclude Ferraris, Rolls Royces and Mercedes.

Prestel is the marriage of industries, technologies, processes and skills which already exist: in telecommunications; the telephone; the computer; and publishing.

Prestel uses the British national telecommunications network, in that computers are installed within it for the Prestel service, and that network is used by the Prestel subscriber to access the computers.

Prestel uses the telephone system because that system already provides access to nearly 60 per cent of British homes and most businesses (and will by AD 2000 probably give as complete a national coverage as a free society will allow); thus the existence of these links makes it economic to provide a new telephone-dependent service.

Prestel uses a modified television set as the terminal device which people can use from their homes to access the service. It does so, once more, because it makes economic sense: television receivers sooner or later have to be replaced (their average life in British society is between nine and eleven years), so why not replace them with a device which has added capability?

The Prestel service as seen by the user gives access to a wide range of data and information, and will lead to an information exchange capability, a message service, and an electronic mail system for home and business use.

The information available on Prestel can be seen from many standpoints: economic, educational, entertainment, social. It will encompass data for which the user pays directly and data brought to him as a public service by society's formal institutions. The information is not provided by the Post Office, but is offered by a wide range of publishers most of whom are already well established in other media, from newspaper and book publishers to consumer protection groups, educational organisations and government bodies. The Post Office in turn acts as publisher, a role in which its minimal expertise will no doubt lead to mistakes as Prestel progresses. But this is normal and to be expected. The message service will make instantaneous written communications possible over a whole society: a type of enormous instantaneous silent telex which enters the living room, yet is under the user's control.

Thus the Prestel package brings together to act in concert economic groupings in society which are unaccustomed to work in association: the Post Office, as provider of digital telecommunications and on-line computer services to a non-professional clientele and as a sort of interface — a publisher without the usual means of control over what is published, yet who shares some of the costs of publication with the ultimate information/data providers; the television manufacturing industry, as manufacturers of a hybrid, a television set which can also accept digital data and act as a communications terminal, turning it from a one-way into a two-way device; and the publishing industry, as providers of electronic-based information which yet appears looking much like print on the television screen; and at the end of the line, the ultimate customer who pays for it by charges based on usage and on whom the exercise stands or falls. For that user will only pay if the services — that is the information — are what he or she wants and are easily (and relatively cheaply) available, or if the total package is so convenient that it becomes the obvious automatic first port of call.

How then are the varying needs of the different parties to be satisfied? For the Post Office, the investment in Prestel is a method of increasing telecommunications and telephone utilisation. For the television industry, Viewdata should increase sales. For publishers it gives other outlets. And for the user? It takes away the mystique and deskills much that was previously done with computing — in other words, it makes computing more widely accessible.

How it works

Basically Prestel, the first of the Viewdata type technology systems, works like this. The television set which the user operates to access the service contains special electronics enabling it to be used either normally or as a Prestel terminal. It is simply connected to the telephone line — by means of a standard jack plug — as well as to the television aerial. The user is provided with a key pad which looks much like a calculator. According to model, the user either dials the computer on his normal telephone handset or, more usually where the key pad has an automatic dialling facility, switches the television receiver on and then dials by pushing the correct button.

Initially the user's controls are all contained in a set of numeric buttons, 0 to 9, and two small control buttons known as Hash (or square) and Star.

The information that the user sees, of which there are many examples in these pages is so organised as to be either in index form with numbers at the side and/or carry page numbers. The user presses the appropriate numeral, followed by one of the control buttons, to activate the frame referred to by the numbers shown. The other control button allows the user to go back a frame without having to remember what was the number of the previous frame or page. Various permutations can be achieved, but this is the basic system.

It sounds simple, and it is. It also sounds limited, but it is not. An immense variety of material can be accessed using simple methods like this. Moreover, this bedrock Model-T service is capable of immense expansion without losing the flexibility that comes with its simplicity. One can add to the television set a range of facilities, present with most existing small computer systems, which expand the capability: alpha numeric keyboards instead of simple numeric pads; tape recorders — so that users can record and play back when not connected; printers for paper output; and more local intelligence within the television set, which will enable the user to manipulate the data received as if the television receiver was also a stand-alone computer, one capable of being used to work as an information retrieval/communications terminal or as a control device, say for reading meters.

What's new?

All the technological means so far mentioned, it will be noticed, already exist. Prestel does not depend on new invention for its arrival, and in some areas there is considerable tried and tested expertise, sometimes in profusion. Like the Model-T Ford, which was largely created by the systematic rearrangement of existing skills and techniques, the keys to Prestel lie in the new economics made possible by the rearrangement, rejigging, and regrouping of skills, some from hitherto very different disciplines and interests.

True, Prestel makes new demands, but again so did the Model-T Ford. A different analogy is that it is in the same class as the Xerox process, similarly starting with the assumption that some of the basics it provides existed before it appeared — that the need was there and had been satisfied, however poorly, before it came along. In the same fashion, people had access to computing power using telecommunications links before Viewdata technology came along, and they used the existing computer systems for information retrieval and message composition and transfer. This still applies, for at the time of writing the public service proper — with real paid for usage — will only be getting into its stride when this book is first published.

What then is new? The newness is a compound of many factors. Before examining them in any detail, it is worth discussing Viewdata at a slightly deeper level than the conceptual marriage of television, telecommunications and computing for the mass market. For Viewdata is not a computer system, an information provision system, or a communications system as these are normally conceived. Instead, it takes certain elements from each and sets out to combine them to create a new medium.

It was not the original intention to create a new medium; that is the by-product, the result. It was the intention to create an information retrieval system for mass-market use, one which would get around the limitations of existing computer systems (complex, skill-demanding, expensive), which excluded them from the mass market. When Viewdata was conceived computer time was still too costly for the washing-machine or even hi-fi markets, and that second market set (at least) was essential were Viewdata to be effective. Viewdata had to be aimed at millions of users, not the thousands which are the norm, and with which the computer industry and community are familiar and at ease.

Now a constant threat to established commercial interests, one visible throughout the history of computing since the early fifties, has been that somewhere in the future lay a wider public which would want computing facilities to do such things as retrieving information — seeking consumer data, scanning encyclopaedias, handling financial and mortgage calculations — and generally accessing the mass of data which existed, but which the existing information-transfer systems of society found impracticable and uneconomic to offer efficiently, which they could not do otherwise given their then existing costs and technology. Moreover, access to such services would not be confined to information retrieval; there were a host of possibilities involving two-way interaction between user and machine systems which could at some time be made economic, if some method of breaking into the mass market could be found.

Of course, services of the kind we are discussing have been in existence for a long time; almost every business of any size has them or access to them. They have been the *raison d'être* for the rise and growth of computing, but they have been aimed at a different market set; direct consumer mass-market economics have been irrelevant. They were available only to members of closed communities, corporations, government departments, universities, or to the corporate customers — usually corporations and businesses — of suppliers of specialist computing services, the customers of the computer bureaux. And they had one important limitation: the aim of both provider and user was usually primarily economic.

When money is at stake — when a user organisation's purpose is economic — it is prepared to pay well for trained staff, or to pay for the staff to be trained. They in turn are prepared to commit time and resources to learning, to acquiring skills. These are normal processes, leading as they have done in engineering, accountancy and architecture to the creation of guilds, unions, and attempts to remove the use of the skills out of the area of normal ken. This process was not really a hindrance in the development of computing, and indeed could be said in part to have accounted for its rise. To impose a body of new skills on society, it is necessary to organise those who possess them to carry the flag, to enthuse, and to show that what they do has both value and scarcity.

But these skills could not be presupposed, inferred or imposed on the consumer mass market; indeed to make that market appear, a Viewdata-like system required a reverse set of design characteristics: the processes would have to be deskilled, and the systems would have to become fault tolerant. What was expensive would have to be made cheap (the computer industry would prefer the term 'inexpensive'); thus the comparison would no longer be with the *Grand Prix* racing car. Additionally, what was to be provided had to go beyond the economic nexus; it also had to be fun or to provide a capacity for fun, and it had to have links to social duty: the webs that keep families, friendships and normal personal business connections together.

To do this, to enter this different area, required that Viewdata be built out of the redevelopment of existing facilities. To use another analogy, Viewdata — even if requiring a small technical jump — had to emulate the electronic calculator which, to be successful, had to replace log tables, slide rules, the abacus and the child's often laboriously constructed examination crib. The need for an easy-to-use facility had to be there, even if before the calculator appeared no-one could see what steps were to be taken to fill it.

It is the same with Viewdata, about which much has already been written. That literature in the main has been concerned with its major elements, particularly the Prestel service and some of the databases that are going on to it. Some of those will be discussed later, showing within one set of covers the range of information that Viewdata systems are capable of handling. At this point, however, it is worth looking at Viewdata in a broader context.

Viewdata & Teletext

We have written that Viewdata is in a class of systems which includes Teletext — sometimes they are all called Teletext. They are so called because they use television or television-like receivers, and work to agreed standards which ensure that what is seen on the screen, in all Teletext systems, will be compatible or can be made so without substantial change. Thus some of the illustrations shown in this book, particularly those which are text only, though of Viewdata-provided information, could be of information provided through other Teletext systems. There are the same colour possibilities, the same maximum number of characters to the line and lines to the screen. However, Teletext systems themselves are part of a broader trend which has quite a long and respectable history. It can be argued indeed that this is one of the major reasons that Viewdata is being so rapidly accepted. For the notion that some sort of system which made use of communications facilities and digital computing would eventually reach into the home has been exhaustively discussed (particularly in the USA) since the middle sixties. We hit only the highlights.

The initial spark was the enthusiasm for what has since become popularly known as 'The Cashless Society', an idea whose limitations are now well known but which attracted a lot of support when first put forward in the early sixties. (The idea in fact has its roots in Science Fiction.) Thus Martin Greenberger, then a computer scientist at MIT, is found foreseeing *(Atlantic Monthly* 1964) terminals linked to an information exchange and universal credit cards as well as terminals in the home used for all the financial transactions that an individual or family engage in: from the preparation of tax documents to the payment of bills and investments on the stock market. In 1966 Douglas Parkhill, then at a leading 'Think Tank', the Mitre Corporation (he went on to become a senior civil servant in Canada and has had much to do with the development of computer communications in that country), wrote what has since become acknowledged as the classic in the field, *The Challenge of the Computer Utility.* In Chapter 8 he considers the uses to which on-line, accessible-to-the-public, mass-market, information-supplying computer systems can be put and ranges much further afield than money. Though dealing with finance, and quoting Greenberger, he discusses shopping from the home — envisaging something similar to the advisory services that the Consumers' Association in the UK are to provide on Prestel. He also looks at other information services. These include legal-, medical-, and educational-data provision. He even has a couple of paragraphs on what he calls automatic publishing, and foresees what has since become known as word processing — now a subset of the existing computer industry, but some parts of which may be possible on Viewdata with later versions of the technology.

The notion that computers and communications were inextricably intertwined, and that this would happen for the general population in the future, became increasingly popular in the late sixties, often under the title 'The Wired Nation'. Most of those writing about it went further than either Greenberger or Parkhill. They were not all simply writers or scientist/consultants. In the boom years of the late sixties, when such studies and writings were all the rage (largely, it must be stated, in America; there was surprisingly little published work in Europe), the Electronics Industries Association, a major US trade body, filed a presentation with the Federal Communications Commission (1969), the US Government Agency which regulates broadcasting, cable and telephone systems. This was in reply to an FCC request for comment on new rules it was proposing for the operation of cable television systems.

The EIA paper was called *The Future of Broadband Communications,* and though mainly concerned with cable systems, it discussed the provision of services which did not require that the country be wired up anew with high-capacity cable, but could use some of the existing facilities. The services included the provision of information, of electronic mail, of data transfer which would then appear in document form. All these facilities can be provided by a Viewdata-type national system, and are expected to be up in the UK within the foreseeable short term.

The general discussion which ensued following this and a host of reports went further than the provision of technology. It also considered the social problems which might arise with its introduction. How, for instance, would the poor be able to afford it all? How would they pay for the new services if these became as essential to life in the USA as the telephone has become? Would there have to be cross-subsidisation as there had been with the telephone system to make its spread into remote areas possible?

In September 1971 another 'Think Tank', the Institute for

the Future in Menlo Park*, California, produced a major report for AT & T, American Telephone & Telegraph, written primarily by one of the smartest men in the communications business, Paul Baran, the initiator of a technology called packet switching. The report is called *The Future of the Telephone Industry*, and its wide canvas sets out to discuss the social background within which the telephone industry will grow and how this might influence the services to be offered. In the section dealing with new services the report again considers cashless-society type transactions, education, mail, answering services, shopping (providing price lists and ordering facilities), fares and ticket reservations, past and forthcoming events listings, banking services, consumer advice, bus, train and air schedules, restaurant data and indexes of the services on offer.

This is the context in which Viewdata has to be set: a background of enquiry, study, interest and belief in the ability of the available technology to provide services seen as socially and economically desirable.

Facilities of Viewdata

However, belief is one thing; achievement is another. To make such services possible the technology had to be put together, which required serious work on the problems involved in obtaining a mass-market system which has generality, which can handle not only the transactions already listed but also those likely to arrive once a system is up and working and people conceive new uses for it.

It is therefore worth looking at the facilities which Viewdata offers, and how these evolved. To do this we have to begin within the general area called software. This area does not only consist of the programs which make Viewdata work and the databases

---

* For anyone wanting a detailed breakdown, the same Institute published three months later *Potential Demand for Two-way Informaiton Services to the Home 1970-1990*, which now makes very instructive reading.

— structured and organised collections of information — that make the system usable, turn it from a collection of inert electronics and mechanics into something useful; just as important and indeed more fundamental, is the collection of architectural ideas which delineate the system's capabilities: the ideas which will organise the system so that the user faces as few constraints as possible. It is within this area that the fundamental decisions are made and the foundations laid.

Now the first essential requirement for a system which is addressed to, and will be addressed by, the widest possible public is that two factors must be balanced.

First, the simple must drive out the complex.

Second, the simplicity itself must close as few doors as possible to future developments and extensions without fundamentally corrupting the system's integrity: it must be possible to graft on some complexity without corruption of the underlying structure.

This is a difficult exercise in balancing.

Initially two major software problems had to be overcome if a system was to be devised which would have mass-market characteristics. The two were interconnected: protocols, and data structure.

Protocols

A protocol in the world of computing/communications has the same exact meaning as in its more widely known field, diplomacy. A protocol is essentially an agreement between all the parties involved that a specific or precise matter (problem) will always be handled and progressed in a just-as-precise, agreed-beforehand-by-all-parties manner. Faced with problem X, all those involved will always do Y.

Drafting protocols so that between them they are all-encompassing is not that easy a task, even if when finally spelt out they seem no more than a set of general principles (see page 40). Unlike most principles however, these are not confined to the unread preamble; they are working principles to be used, principles against which ideas and developments to be incorporated are first tested.

When adhered to, they have one particular effect: the road down which they guide you leads to quite specific operational conclusions. It needs to be emphasised however that in arriving at a simple system, you could also arrive at an *unnaturally* simple system; one requiring the learning of a routine which though simple is not generally near instinctive. A system can be questioned in many ways. The way chosen (which the examples onwards illustrate) with Viewdata is so widely and generally used that it is no longer thought of as a methodology but rather as almost a part of the human psyche.

The result is that once the user has learnt to use the few controls, the only problems he/she can have in operating Viewdata are those caused by the effects of the learning curve, or by 'butter fingers'. Given that the data or facilities sought are present in the system, that the rules have been observed when setting up the data or service; that the system is operational; that the user is connected and able and willing to pay; then the user should never be unable to find a way through the system.

The protocols in turn almost force the data to be structured in a particular basic way: *a hierarchic tree structure.*

Data structure

Conceptually, a hierarchic tree is the most basic of structures. It has linear characteristics in that, when properly described, one step can almost inexorably follow another, the proper description coming from the rigid use of the appropriate protocols. It has a regularity across all subject matter. Given a good indexing scheme, it can be used to handle immense complexity. Moreover, if the indexing scheme is numeric and you know the required number, you can go directly to the information you seek.

So why are all data not handled in this way? Because it is not all-inclusive. The majority of data structures in computing have some hierarchic connotations to them, but they are organised

So why are all data not handled in this way? Because it is not all-inclusive. Most data structures in computing have some hierarchic connotations to them, but they are organised according to a particular set of operational requirements. The complexity and variety of those requirements has meant that there are a number of approaches, and just as much *ad hoc* development without thought of basic structure to get some specific application to work and run. So we have a situation in which there are many theories, many different ways of structuring, and many different systems built to enable specifics to be run, but as yet no generally accepted standard, all-pervading principles. This means that, given the same enquiry about similar items within two collections of data on two systems, you may well take a different set of steps and follow a different route through the data in each system, though the end result to the user may look identical.

The hierarchic data structure which Viewdata uses may be simple, but in an information-retrieval role its power is considerable. It can only be illustrated in part for the structure goes down nine levels,. and as each point in each level has ten choices beneath it, at level nine a thousand million options are available.

This does not mean to say that you must necessarily fill one hundred million parts of the structure before you go to level 9. All that you need do is consider the structure as a matrix on which data is hung. What is important is the vertical chain, the ability to go from one piece of data to another increasing the specificity at each step.

What we are considering here of course is not data as one individual item, one piece of information. Each of the potential choices, — there are 900 million of them within the nine-level hierarchic tree in Prestel — consists of one screenful of data when seen on the receiver and sometimes several continuation pages. It does not follow that the screen has to be full; it does follow that this is all that needs to be stated about an item at that level, which can usefully sit on that frame.

Frames

Now it may well be that the item in fact takes up more space than the screen can display. This is quickly overcome by producing one or more connecting (horizontally in terms of the data structure) frames and listing them in the identification which any item carries as following that particular frame.*

One can get some understanding of what a frame can convey by considering the existing screen's designed capacity: twenty-four lines, each forty characters in length. If you then make allowances for the loss of two lines (one at the top to give the frame reference number and/or other control information, and one at the bottom on which to state instructions as to what the user should do next), and for spacing between words on an average word length of five characters, you have a message-length possibility of around 145 to 150 words each frame, without using large capitals.

In stating this of course, we give a current immediate Viewdata limitation. A standard business letter within much of European culture is of the order of two to three hundred words, which would require two frames, with the flicking back and forth that this implies. However, this is not an ultimate Viewdata-system limitation; it is an immediate limitation arising from the existing screen technology on the market and will eventually change as the receivers are expanded to eighty characters a line, which is likely to happen in the mid-eighties.

Characteristics of Viewdata

Simple to use

At this point, you may well wish to retrace a step and ask why, if the hierarchic structure is so simple yet so powerful that it takes very few steps to dig deeply, it is not yet a standard for the

---

* They are referred to as frames or pages, and the two will be used here according to context, a frame being what you see at any time, a page being an item which may take more than one frame.

arrangement of all data. The reason is simple: Viewdata is being constructed in the expectation that all data will be used directly, and that no operational data has more value than any other.

Much of the data in commercial computer systems is not of that order. It is dependent upon other data and will never surface outside the system except as part of a conclusion or an answer, or as an item which was one among many from which the conclusion, the trend line, the average or the total was drawn.

Thus, the limited Viewdata requirement has in turn led to a major difference between Viewdata operating software and that of most conventional commercial systems operating software. The latter usually is constructed to enable a class of questions to be asked: that class of questions does not comprise all the possible questions that the data's collection could lead to: some indeed are never asked as they are not seen as having value. However, even to ask a quite simple set of questions, and to set up a not-very-large variety of question-answering routines across a substantial collection of data can lead to quite complex software, a wide range of cross-connections to be set up temporarily and then to be re-set with different paths to ask the next question.

This is not the requirement with Viewdata, and the software complexity is avoided. Indeed, to go any other route would cut against the protocols, the agreements devised to make sure that the system has as wide generality and availability as possible. The protocols would then have to become more complex, there would be more to memorise, more to search the instruction manual for, to ask what the next move should be, and Viewdata would drift away from what can be described as its prime directive: that there should be no more instructions (indeed in many cases not even as many!) as are found to operate a washing machine. Complexity would mean more to go wrong, perhaps a need for an instruction manual. For though a few leaflets might be produced, there is unlikely to be what could be called a *Viewdata Instruction Manual*. Indeed, it was absolutely essential to Viewdata that no instruction manual should be required, that a child should be able to use it without more than minimal instruction, that such instruction should be provided by the system and at that clearly and unambiguously.

Meeting these requirements has resulted in a simple-to-use system; the prerequisites for turning computing power from the tool of the trained specialist to the tool — the plaything — of the layman. But though these considerations lie at the heart of Viewdata, they were not the only prerequisites. It was essential that the communications capability was also standard and could be widely used, and that the terminal device should grow out of facilities with which the public were familiar.

Compatible with familiar existing systems

The same sort of thinking was applied. Firstly, Viewdata, in line with the Post Office requirement that whatever was devised was to utilise the existing telecommunications network, is based on the telephone system. Secondly, the terminal requirement is met by the modification of the existing television receiver.

But why should the British Post Office management require that anything devised must utilise the telephone system? Because that system in Britain is in the main drastically underloaded outside business hours. The problem which faced management and which has increasingly worried it since the heavy modernisation investment programme began in the late sixties, was that phone usage in the UK is depressingly low. (It is not that high on average anywhere else either.) The problem can be put quite simply and starkly: Post Office investment in additional telecommunications facilities in 1978 was running at around £900 million a year. By contrast, the home telephone user made an average one and a half calls a day.

Meanwhile the Post Office was committed to introduce digital switching technology with its greater potential reliability and better performance, and was also heading in the direction of different transmission technologies, digital and switched, which would eventually result in an improved utilisation of the telephone system. Yet here was a system which could be developed to make use of the phone network as it stood, and which, in the initial build-up periods, could be placed within exchanges which could carry the load, yet was also a system easily able to be accommodated by the new technology, and capable of further development and expansion in line with it, one which might lead people to make greater use of the telephone-telecommunications system.

Now Viewdata is essentially a digital system: all data transmission is in this form, even if with current analogue technology one has to use means of digital conversion. Transmission of digital data over analogue networks can cause problems, but these are problems we are able to cope with, even if there has to be extra user — as well as carrier — expense. The user will require special interfacing equipment, known as a modem (for modulate-demodulate) which is placed at both ends of the line and which makes data look like speech, as far as the telephone system is concerned. Such equipment has not in the past been exactly cheap, at least when compared with the average telephone rental. This is partly because of the method of manufacture: modems built on traditional lines, out of what are called discrete components (which usually have to be part hand-assembled during modem manufacture) can be quite complex devices to construct, requiring a considerable number of circuits to be created, for which the parts have to be obtained and boxed.

Viewdata, however, was created at a time of rapid change in components technology, the growth of the silicon-based, integrated-circuit industry which enabled what would sometimes be hundreds of discrete components to be replaced by simple, small, low-power requirement, integrated circuits which carried out the same functions but could be produced cheaply and by mass-production methods.

The result is that the modem as we have understood it in the past has been overtaken by events: what was previously a quite substantial black box, a separate collection of electronics, could now be put up on one printed-circuit board, which in

Introduction 19

turn could be inserted into a transmission/reception device quite easily and simply. So why not in Viewdata receivers? That in turn could lead to substantial change on the market. But the Post Office here went one step further. It has in the past insisted that modems would in the main come from itself — as it was entitled to do by the Act of Parliament which established the Post Office as a corporation. (There were certain exceptions in higher transmission speeds.) The Post Office now agreed that, for the purposes of Viewdata, manufacturers would be able to devise and install modem circuits into the terminal devices, i.e. the modified domestic television set, they would sell directly to the public.

Visual display terminal

But what devices? It was obvious that the phone with voice output and a dial input would not be enough. Indeed had the telephone alone been a serious contender, it is unlikely that the Post Office would have given permission for others to provide integrated modems for direct sale. It was obvious also, that the telephone line connection to the subscriber, if not the instrument, was the key to more effective use of the telecommunications network.

Voice then would not do, even were computerised voice response to be an economic reality for the mass market, which as yet it is not. But there was another reason why voice would not do: it was seen that in introducing computing services into the phone network, another major characteristic of the computer could be brought into play. This is its store and forward capability — the capacity of a computer system to accept an input, prepare a response, and either transmit that response or hold it till the terminal to which it is addressed is free and accessible.* (This has considerable implications, dealt with in greater detail in a number of chapters, notably Chapter 3).

There were two routes open to the Post Office. One was to go down the standard computer terminal route, to try to get

---

* Though it would be possible to do this with voice, it made more sense to do it with a device people could see.

users to accept that they could have the service if they bought a special-purpose device, probably a terminal based on visual display technology, the technology of the electron tube. The problem here was that the price levels were too high for the home market if such a display were to be based on the standard computer terminal products. Even with mass-production volumes, the best economic forecasts did not foresee that public disposable income (for which in any case there was much competition) would be large enough to guarantee a mass market. No mass market, no Viewdata, for without that mass-market possibility the investment in the extra facilities required for Viewdata could not be economically justified.

The dilemma indeed was classic: for there to be a service offering information to a mass market, there had to be enough terminals in place, and for those terminals to be in place, not only had the price to be right, there had to be enough facilities and services available for people to invest in the terminal.

Impasse? Well, not really, for in the other route there was already a device in the home, also based on the electron tube, which could be adapted and turned into a digital terminal. What is more it was a robust device and the mass-production industry required to produce it was already in existence.

Like the USA, the British television receiver market is saturated. Unlike the USA, however, the British television receiver market is not one hundred per cent sales to the public. Instead, over 50 per cent of the market is held by rental companies who purchase in bulk and then rent out sets for public use. (This is the result of being early: when mass television began in the fifties, sets were expensive when compared with the then UK disposable income, and tube life was not thought to be high. So the mass television service receiver market base was initially largely built on rental.)

When Viewdata was conceived, this had to be taken into account and indeed was seen as a bonus. Initially it was thought that the Viewdata service would appeal to the rental companies, who would gradually replace end-of-life sets with Viewdata sets and thus encourage the customer to trade up. This would help to quickly achieve a sufficiency of terminals out on the market to launch a mass service.

It is not, however, turning out quite like that. Among the early moves made by the Post Office was to decide that Viewdata and Teletext would be compatible, as far as the television display was concered, thus avoiding a proliferation of standards and making it easy for the TV industry to produce the new sets. Although Teletext display standards had some limitations, these were accepted for the sake of compatibility.

Here then was a manufacturing industry faced with one new set of standards for two services. It was also (and is still) faced with a situation in which market saturation and foreign competition (particularly from Japan) had combined to turn the industry from one in which production lines could be run optimally and profitably to one in decline. Production cutbacks and plant closures had occurred, and the future did not exactly inspire confidence. The problem that faced the UK television set manufacturers was simple: unless and until someone came up with an entirely radical and new colour-television technology, one promising performance of a different order from that already out on the market, enough improved performance to make it a mass production product, they saw no way of increasing production sufficiently to get themselves out of trouble.

As things stood they were partly in the hands of the rental companies who, in the economic conditions of the mid-seventies, were not ordering in any quantity. The industry had assumed a product life of nine to eleven years for a receiver; it was beginning to look like eleven to thirteen or even more, and to make things worse an increasing share of the direct sales market, particularly the small second-set market, was going to Japanese companies and importers of products built in such apparently unlikely havens of high technology as South Korea.

So, unless there were to be a new type of service based on the home colour television receiver which had mass-market appeal, the problems were likely to continue. And this was not just a UK problem. It was also, for instance, a French, West German, Benelux and US problem. Add that the television set was a passive reception instrument and that the manufacturers had little or no influence on broadcasting and the availability of services, and they were in a weak position.

The information industry

What they needed were allies, which with Viewdata is what they obtained. Viewdata might initially be conceived as an information-retrieval service but it was quickly seen by both of us — one as inventor, the other as reporter/observer — that it was the Xerox situation all over again; the difference was that it soon became apparent that Viewdata did not suffer the initial Xerox (Haloid) Corporation problems. Indeed, far from investment capital avoiding it till proven, with Viewdata it has very quickly come on board.

Firstly, the Post Office, after some initial internal argument at the top, soon saw that Viewdata could become a major service.

Secondly, a group of existing corporations, between them substantial economic powers in the land, foresaw that Viewdata or some similar system could be a major tool for dissemination of information, and that what could be done for a nationwide market could also work for parts of it; that the Prestel/Viewdata system, though conceived as a mass-market public information retrieval service, was not inherently limited to this and could be permutated in many different ways, among them special Viewdata services aimed at groups of society with like minds and interests who would pay a premium for specialised information if they could obtain it quickly enough, or in the fast developing jargon of the fast-growing Viewdata professional community, closed user groups (see page 121). And Viewdata-compatible systems could be built for use within organisations (see page 125). This gave three starting possibilities: access to a public service; access to closed user groups on payment of the membership fees; and internal to organisation services closed entirely to the outside world.

The corporations we are discussing could be considered between them as constituting the information industry. They included publishers of all kinds; education services; the management services organisations of large corporations; the computing industry generally; hardware and software services and bureaux; and a substantial part of the electronics industry, particularly that involved in consumer electronics: television, radio and so on.

And what they and almost everyone else realised was that the television manufacturer could now forecast not simply the next generation of television product, the product which would obsolesce the existing television set, but could foresee at least the generation after that.*

The possible change comes from an alteration in the 'nature' of the television receiver, hitherto a passive one-way transmission product, into a two-way traffic station, one with which the user interacts. And of course once you can achieve this, you can build services based on the individual nature of users and their requirements: you give them a capability to specify what those requirements are.

As it stands, even with the addition of the modem and decoding devices, and numerical and control keyboard, the Viewdata equipped television receiver has little local intelligence. Unlike today's computer terminals, what you can do with it is restricted. However, using microprocessor technology it would not be difficult to add such intelligence. It would be possible too to add local storage, a full keyboard (numeric and alpha) and printed paper output.

All these things are already on the way. Indeed, Viewdata's timing could not have been better: the standard tape cassette was rapidly becoming a cheap method of data storage in the burgeoning small business systems and home computing market. Microprocessor and storage prices were continuing to tumble and the processor itself continually improving in performance. And small cheap printers were under intensive development for other mass markets.

---

* One might agree with George Kennan that some problems should be left for one's grandchildren to settle: nevertheless, there are possibilities for change inherent in Viewdata-equipped receivers, enough of which can be foreseen at the time of writing to make it likely that those production lines can keep going at least up to the year 2000.

We can summarise what has happened quite quickly. There is now a rapidly growing interaction between the Post Office, the manufacturers, and the third element in the new grouping, the information industry or Information Providers ('IPs', in the jargon of the growing Viewdata industry).

Among the basic decisions made by the Post Office in its attempt to launch Viewdata was one just as fundamental to its future as the change in the nature of the TV set, from a receiver of TV broadcasts to an interactive data-receiver which Viewdata has brought the manufacturer. The Post Office early decided that it would not become involved in the business of information provision: it was not equipped to do so, and it would require a major investment were it to try to turn itself into a provider of databases; an activity which would also be fraught with political difficulties, not least accusations of 'Big Brother'. Instead it decided that subject to the normal British obscenity and libel laws the Viewdata service would be transparent. The PO would provide the computing, network and line facilities, and the operational software to run the system; the information would be provided on a normal commercial risk basis by outside companies who would pay a storage charge, would have to format their data according to clearly laid down rules, and would obtain their revenue from the users (through the PO, who would act as revenue collector) on the basis of usage — the greater the use, the greater the return.

The Post Office would charge the user an access to the system on a time basis, plus the cost of a local phone call. The IP would specify an additional charge per frame to cover his costs and profit, which the Post Office would collect on his behalf at the same time as collecting the access charge.

The Post Office's reasoning was very good; To appreciate how good it was we have to go back once more into the history of computing. That mass services could arise from computing had been foreseen since it began, but somehow the technology or the costs had never before been right for the mass home market, and the few attempts actually to bring out digital services for public use had so far been unsuccessful. (Perhaps

Introduction 25

the best-known example of this was the addition of digital services to the US Picturephone Service of AT & T, withdrawn when Picturephone itself was withdrawn.)

Yet side by side with this, the newspaper and journal publishers, the publishers of directories and the like have seen the growth of computation, and have noted how their own organisations could in part be switched to selling their data and information via digital services, were such services to be an economically attractive proposition. They have watched as digital techniques have begun to spread within their commercial organisation, and have realised that it was just a matter of time and someone's initiative before such mass-market services appeared.

Some of course have been attempting to make the transition before Viewdata came along: on-line databases providing data previously handled by other means are now common, but they are still skill-demanding, expensive and restricted. Many publishers use computer techniques to produce books, journals, directories; some indeed are no more than computer print bound and sold as if they were conventionally produced books. But all along, they have known that these uses were on the periphery, though they have also realised that it was no more than a matter of time before they became central.

Now suddenly with Viewdata they can see a vehicle: the mass-market information distribution system in embryo. Is it any wonder that, with the Post Office promising transparency to anyone prepared to pay its proposed charges, many of those in the business of mass-market information provision are hurrying to become IPs and gearing themselves to provide a Prestel Viewdata service? For of course the normal commercial ground rules are going to operate; those with existing information gathering, sorting and production organisations have an edge, and the first organisations to provide data and a service stand more chance of making their Prestel Viewdata operation a success than those coming in later. Besides which, the existence of a specific, listed-information service will deter competitors, who rather than putting up the data covering the same ground and aimed at

ABC Travel Guides	Extel
Ackrill Group	Financial Times
James Adams & Associates	General Dental Council
Agricultural Cooperating & Marketing Services	Glass's Guide
	Guinness Superlatives
AP-Dow Jones	Horserace Totalisator Board
Barclaycard	Imperial College of Science & Technology
Benn Brothers	
Birmingham Post & Mail	Industrial Commodities Exchange
British Airways	
British Farm Produce Council	The Institute of Electrical Engineers (INSPEC)
British Gas	
British Printing Corporation	Institute for Scientific Information
Campaign for Real Ale	
Careers & Occupational Information Centre	IPC
	Link House Group
Central Office of Information	London Borough of Hackney
Citizens Advice Brueau	London Borough of Hammersmith
Consumers Association	
Council for Educational Technology	London Borough of Lambeth
	London Borough of Waltham Forest
Datastream International	
Fergus Davidson Associates	London Transport
Eastern Counties Newspapers	Meteorological Office
Electricity Council	Milton Keynes Development Corporation
English Tourist Board	
Exchange & Mart	National Book League

the same interests may well look elsewhere. To put it simply, the first in any field are quite likely to have that field to themselves for some time to come, and what is more are likely to put up data which they are reasonably certain they can handle and support; i.e. it will be central to their information resources. Two examples on Prestel immediately spring to mind. The *Guinness Book of Records* is putting up its major resource, the data on which the book is based. Extel, providers

National Buildings Agency
National Council of
 Social Service
National Gardens Scheme
National Gas Consumer
 Council
National Savings
National Trust
National Audio Visual Aids
 Centre
New Opportunity Press

The Open University
Optical Information Council
Parkers Guide
Professional Association of
 Teachers
PIRA
PO Data Transmission
 Service
PO Directories
PO Experiment in Education
PO External Telecommuni-
 cations Executive
PO Giro
PO Postal
PO Telephones

PO Wales and Marches
 Telecommunications Board
Department of Prices and
 Consumer Protection
Quantas Airways

Radio Society of Great
 Britain
Reuters
Royal Horticultural Society
Royal National Institute for
 the Deaf

WH Smith
South Eastern Newspapers
Sports Council
Sportsdata
St Albans College
St James Press

The Stock Exchange
Technical Indexes Ltd
Training Services Agency
Transport & Road Research
 Laboratory
Universities Central Council
 on Admissions
Westminster Press

of financial data and long-time suppliers of company information (their best-known and most widely used product probably being the Extel company card), are preparing initially a short form of that card.

A listing of the companies and organisations which had signed contracts with the Post Office (as of July 1977) is worth studying. They are listed alphabetically in the box above.

It is important to realise that this list is an early one, before

Viewdata had had much public exposure. A number of strands are immediately apparent. First, there is a preponderance of publishers, both of newspapers and of magazines and reference books: most of the major UK units are present. Next are the major nationalised utilities, gas, electricity, and the offshoots of government — even if far removed from traditional government — whose work has an in-built information function: British Airways, the English Tourist Board, the General Dental Council, and the Meteorological Office. The government too is directly and well represented by, among others, the COI and the Department of Prices and Consumer Protection.*

However, what does stand out is that the list is crammed with national bodies which are only loosely government related, supported usually by private funds and subscriptions, yet which have a national information role to play, from the National Book League and the Radio Society of Great Britain, to the Optical Information Council and the Royal Horticultural Society.

It is noticeable that in some cases the basic and immediate data in a particular market sector will be provided on Viewdata by the preponderance of those within that sector of the information provision industry: indeed in some cases of narrow market sectors (of which the *Guinness Book of Records* is an example) 100 per cent of the production end of the market sector is involved with Viewdata, while in areas not so narrow, such as the provision of up-to-date financial information, the inclusion of Extel, the *Financial Times* and AP-Dow Jones takes in the major parties in the market.§

We have so far been discussing the background to Viewdata, the rationale for its appearance which will ensure its success as a mass-market, information-retrieval service. Before we move on to consider Viewdata in its differing roles, and in more detail, it is essential to return to the question of Teletext and the international dimension of Viewdata. We have written that

---

* Now subsumed in The Department of the Environment
§ Extel and the F.T. have joined together for this purpose forming a new company called Fintel.

Viewdata is Teletext compatible and given some idea of the rationale behind the decision to make it so. Now Teletext itself is a broadcast system, a non-interactive system in that all the information it provides is preprogrammed, put into the broadcast sequence, and the user merely waits until the required data come around. The user may not know that this is the process that is going on, only seeing on the screen the data called for, but as Teletext is a closed-loop system in which all data is broadcast in sequence, this is what does happen. The system may be controlled by a keyboard similar to that used in Viewdata, but Viewdata it is not. Teletext then does not call for the technical facilities of Viewdata: however in terms of character size, number of lines, etc., Viewdata and Teletext initially look identical to the user. This may seem somewhat restrictive, but there is little restriction that human ingenuity cannot overcome. More important is that a Teletext standard has been agreed and accepted, which should ensure that national systems incompatible to Prestel Viewdata will not appear in the UK. (This does not of course mean that there could not be national networks devised using Viewdata type technology which are made incompatible *by design*. But these would be private networks, the incompatibility being one way of helping to ensure security and privacy.)

It also means that there is a standard in one country behind which those involved can rally, their combined impetus giving a much greater chance of being able to hold the line when faced — as we probably will be — on the international market with standards which are different, because they originate with systems being built elsewhere.*

This could be important to its future, for Viewdata is already becoming international. The software has been sold to the West German Telephone Authority, the Bundespost, which is preparing a service of its own, aided by IT & T (International Telephones and Telegraphs) one of whose

---

* The clash has already occured. The French have a system under development called ANTIOPE which operates according to different standards. Steps have already been taken at international meetings to work out methods of reconciliation so that what appears on ANTIOPE could in the long term also appear on Viewdata type systems.

subsidiaries is working on the software conversion and on receiver design.

Viewdata packages, software hardware and expertise, have also been sold to the Dutch PTT, the Hong Kong telephone company, and to Switzerland. INSAC, the British software export company which has the US rights to British Viewdata technology, has come to an agreement with one of America's larger communications companies, GT & T to introduce Viewdata-type systems into the US market, systems expected to be launched in late 1979.

One can expect then that in the early eighties, publicly accessible Viewdata systems will be in operation on both sides of the Atlantic, as well as in Asia. (Even the Chinese People's Republic has been showing interest, having sent delegations to look at the experiments being conducted in Hong Kong.) And coming up is the 'superset' Viewdata system, the possibility of eventually being able to access data internationally. This should be distinguished from a different system also under development, Prestel Internation, the PO's attempt with other parties to make Prestel data available internationally, sometimes to countries which may not have a Viewdata system at all, but from which some terminal access is possible.

But what will be done with these public services? We take for our examples services and data developed in Britain for Prestel and other Viewdata technology systems. Not because there is no interesting work done elsewhere, for there is, but because it is the system we know best, and — perhaps more important — Britain is further advanced in the development than other countries.

Viewdata as a public service has two basic uses: information retrieval and electronic mail. Of the two, it may well be that the second will in the long term be more important, a galaxy sized market as opposed to the planet sized market for information retrieval. However, the British service begins with information retrieval, and this is, so far, where the majority of experience has been gained. It is with this therefore that we begin our description proper.

2   Information retrieval

It is essential to understand that Viewdata was initially designed for the dissemination of a very large and wide-ranging collection of information: this lay at the heart of the design and was the key to the concept. The information to be provided had to range as widely as possible not because anyone had delusions of grandeur, but for reasons of economics. Viability, it was seen, rested on providing so many information options that though each individual sector of the Viewdata database might only have a small user population, the total system would command a sufficiently wide readership to make the system attractive to a mass-market service provider, then seen as the management of the Post Office. It is the old story: just as much management effort is required to create and manage a potentially £100-million operation as one which will run at £1000 million or more.

It was soon found that the generality of Viewdata was such that additional services could be hung on and around it. Viewdata would involve a network of distributed computer systems, each near to or within a major population centre. The computer systems however need not be restricted to information retrieval. It should therefore be possible to add other services within the capability of computers embedded in a communications network, not least among them services which the computing community would regard as traditional, particularly where these required a mix of computing and telecommunications. In addition there was the whole range of communications services made possible by the store and forward capability of that technological mix: message transmission services ranging in reaction speed from real time to overnight, and conversational services. But see Chapter 3.

It is this spread which sets Viewdata apart from existing computer-based systems. The rationale underlying the Viewdata concept determined the protocols and access methods, the style of which can be inferred from the first paragraph of this chapter. Very little further thought is needed to arrive at the 'flavour' of the initial system. If the prerequisites for mass-market operations are simplicity of operation and ease of use, a wide-ranging database, and economics based on a large number of database options — each of which is likely to interest a large section of the possible total user population, and many of which will at some time appeal to the entire user population — then the components of that immediately obvious database can be relatively easily listed.

The examples below are selected from the initial Viewdata listing. All were in the 'first edition'. (Most are in some form in the current edition.)

Buying a Car	Financial Information
An Evening Out	Market Intelligence
Houses for Sale	Business Intelligence
Local Information	Community Service
Social Guidance	Route Planning
Looking for a Job	Holiday Information
Entertainment	News
Education	Sports Results

Probably the best way to illustrate how Viewdata is used in information retrieval (apart from exposure to the system itself) is to go through the operations required to search a specific interest section of the database. The example we pick is the first on the list above: 'Buying a Car'

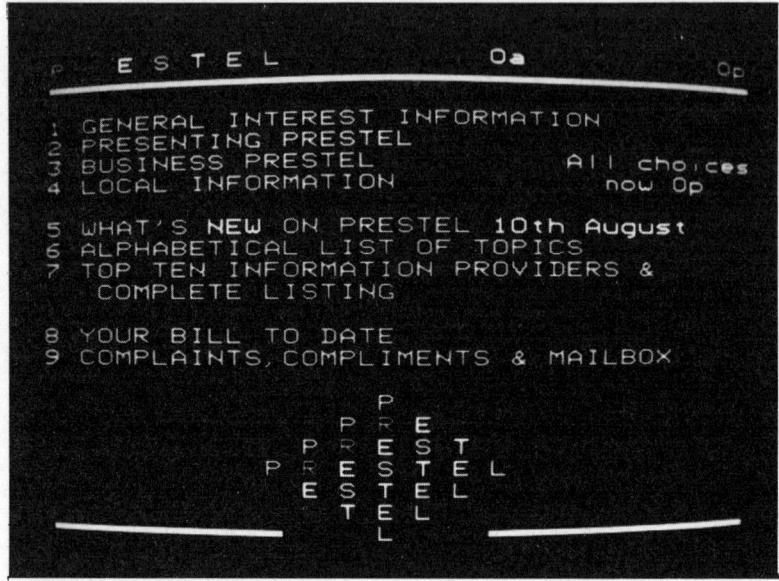

'Buying a Car'

This is a useful example to choose because the purchase of a car using existing media is an operation capable of extension almost to infinity. It is possible for Viewdata to reflect the range of would-be purchasers and their style of operation, which can range from, 'We'll have that' (first choice available) to, 'Let's look at all models available at all prices in all colours'.

On entering Viewdata, the first page on offer is the main index, page 0, which lists services available, and under the first choice, which is the widest, comes a brief list of the topics covered.

On page 1 for example is found information on Holidays, Travel, Employment, Entertainment, Sport and Hobbies, etc. A prompt at the bottom of the page tells the user to key the choice required on the keypad. It is a feature of the system that every page has a prompt, which indicates the user's next action if he/she is to continue. It will be noted that another heading in page 0 offers the user the choice of seeking the information required by reference to the alphabetical index.

Information retrieval 35

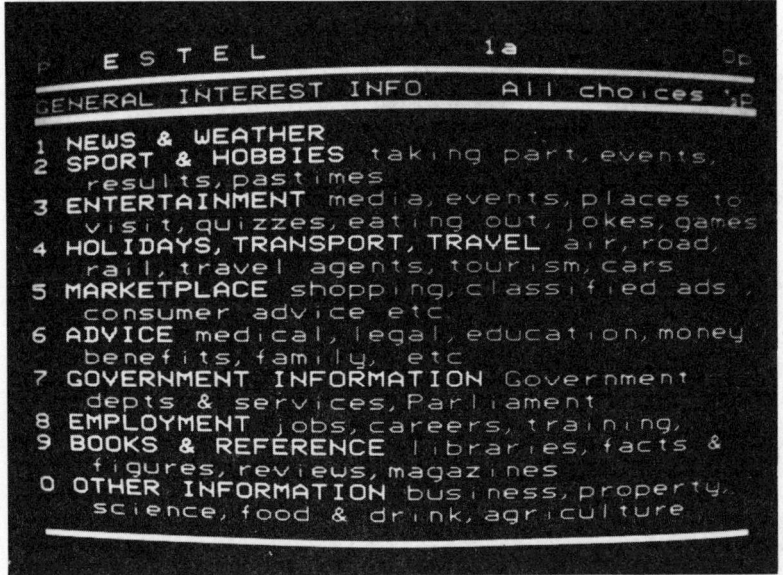

On keying 4 Viewdata offers the next page, page 14. Here 'Cars & Motoring' is choice 5. Keying 5 calls the index of the 'Cars & Motoring' section, page 143, which lists topics relating to cars: Motoring Advice, Buying a Car, Motor Sport, etc. One of the headings under choice 2 is 'Car Buying Guide'. Thus, by keying a single digit at every page the user is able to home on, for instance, a complete report on the Jaguar XJ car, as shown in the sequence (detailed on pages 36-7).

The 'Car Buying Guide' (page 1432) lists eight sources of information on the buying of cars: *Motoring Which?*, *Autocar* and *Exchange & Mart*, etc. The user may at this stage select one of the sources, say in this instance *Motoring Which?* (choice 1) and possibly go back to page 1432 later, to explore the other choices. This is a good illustration of system flexibility and user control.

So far the page numbers (shown on the top right-hand side of each frame) have gone through the sequence of choices made; page 1432 was obtained by first keying 1, then 4, then 5

```
P  E S T E L             14a     0
  TRAVEL  HOLIDAYS  TRANSPORT
  1 RAIL TRAVEL ½p Timetables,historic
    lines,rail/hover/sea timetables
  2 AIR TRAVEL ½p International & UK
    internal flights
  3 OTHER TRANSPORT ½p Travel agents,
    river & sea transport,shipping
  4 HOLIDAYS & TOURISM ½p Holidays
    available,accommodation,guides to
    places to visit,advice,complaints
  5 CARS & MOTORING ½p Motoring advice,
    routes,car buying,motoring holidays,
    motor sport
  6 BUSINESS TRAVEL ½p
  7 HOTELS ½p
  8 INFORMATION FOR TRAVEL BUSINESSES ½p
  9 INFORMATION FOR OVERSEAS VISITORS ½p
  0 INFORMATION ON FOREIGN COUNTRIES ½p
  $
```

and finally 2. On selecting 1 in the 'Car Buying Guide' on page 1432 the user is directed to page 3333, which is the gateway to the data allocated to *Motoring Which?* Once in this area a number of alternatives are offered which can lead to the specific information required; on page 33339 (obtained by keying 1 first, then 9) the user is offered a choice of alphabetically classified car reports. Reports on the Jaguar — and other cars in the same alphabetic grouping — are under choice 5. Finally, choice 1 homes in on the Jaguar XJ (page 3333940) which gives a brief verdict on the car and a list of related items of further information, again with page numbers, which the user may obtain by keying the numbers listed.

One of the first points to note from the above sequence is that every page has on the top right-hand side a page number, followed by a letter, identifying the page on display. Pages of information may consist of one or more continuation frames, thus subsequent frames of the same page are given the same number as the parent page but with sequential letters of the alphabet, a to z.

Information retrieval

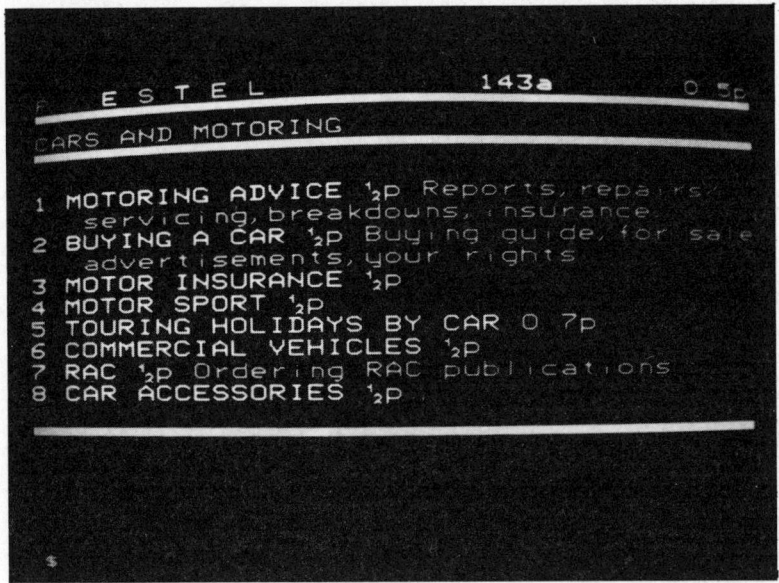

It is important to understand the flexibility with which the top-line of the screen frame identification can be used. In the UK Prestel system some of the pages will have 'Prestel' marked on the top left-hand side, while others in the sequence illustrated have *Which?* The former are the lead-in pages provided by the Post Office to guide the user to the data area required, while the latter are provided by the Information Provider (in this case *Motoring Which?*) who is responsible for the entry contents, their accuracy, relevance and updating.

Search methods?

The method of selection illustrated is known as 'treeing down the database'. Two other methods are also available but they must be used in conjunction with the treeing method and rely on the existence of a subject directory and an Information Provider directory (both supplied free to the UK user). With these aids, the user can find the gateway page number (in the above example page 1432 is the gateway to the

'Car Buying Guide', or alternatively the gateway to *Motoring Which?* page 3333), after which the normal treeing method is used.

Given the page number of the gateway, Viewdata provides the means of jumping direct to it by keying page no., thus by-passing the lead-in pages, and also obviously saving time and additional charge.

There are other ways of increasing the pace of the information retrieval process, and avoiding the treeing down routine. One is based on the use of a model of the tree structure stored in the Viewdata *computer* (it could also be stored in a microprocessor associated with the Viewdata *receiver*), searched automatically to retrieve a page number corresponding with a keyword or set of keywords. Again *Motoring Which?* is a good example to use. Here on activating the model, for example by keying 'Find Jaguar XJ data', it would reach down to the particular heading of the data item required (in this example, 'Jaguar XJ') and would automatically call up the page from store.

Clearly there are problems in implementing search arrangements of this kind if at the same time it is desired that users be able to handle the searches without complicated training. It is unlikely that sophisticated search methods will be suitable for most home users — at least in the next few years — not only due to the inherent training difficulties, but also because they will probably be more costly than allowing the user to make his own search which effectively makes more intensive use of the user's abilities (to make the selection at every stage) and less intensive use of the system's power. The machine search may initially appear to be more sophisticated, but is in fact considerably less so since the system cannot be provided with a natural language dialogue recognition capability, and neither does the user have to understand a specialised set of instructions, which the computer has been programmed to understand, to make enquiries.

It is worth noting the freedom which this system affords the user: to dwell as long as he wishes on any of the pages on display; to recall any of the previous pages examined (currently

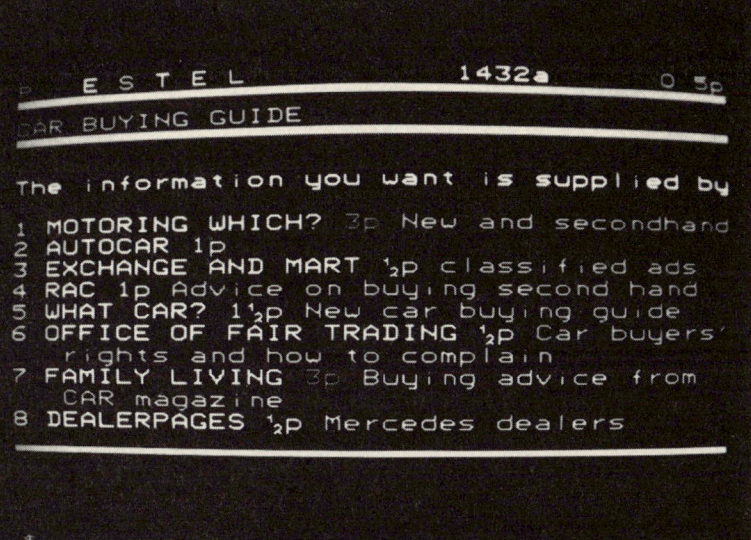

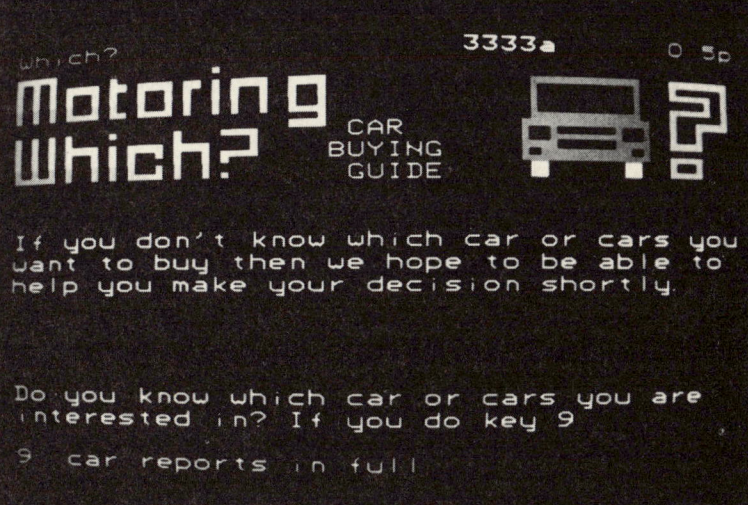

up to a maximum of four) by using the simple command * # ; to retransmit a page being displayed if he suspects that it has been corrupted in transmission by keying *00; and finally to correct a keying error, when jumping to a named page, by keying **. With this simple set of instructions — usually found engraved on the keypad — a user can learn to 'drive' Viewdata very quickly.

Another aspect of the system worthy of note is the opportunity it opens for serendipity. Indeed this is an important argument against using apparently refined and powerful search methods which, though appearing more efficient, reduce considerably the chances of finding useful information which one is unable to define sufficiently well for systematic and/or powerful computer organised search methods to be applied.

Examples of the above are shown on page 1432 where a choice is given of three sources of car reports, which the browser might not have known about (page 333394 and the following page). These open up information which the user who was directed straight to 'Jaguar XJ' (possibly further refined to bring up a specific aspect of the car) might not otherwise have discovered.

'An Evening Out'

> *'Let's get out of here.'*
> *'What are we going to do?'*
> *'I don't know: what are we going to do?'*
> *'I don't know either. You tell me. What are we going to do?'*
> *'Aw. Come on. What are we going to do?'*

The above now classic dialogue is not the sole preserve of teenagers, who if they knew what they were going to do would probably change their minds anyway. *Acidie* is part of the human condition and no-one should expect new media to change that.

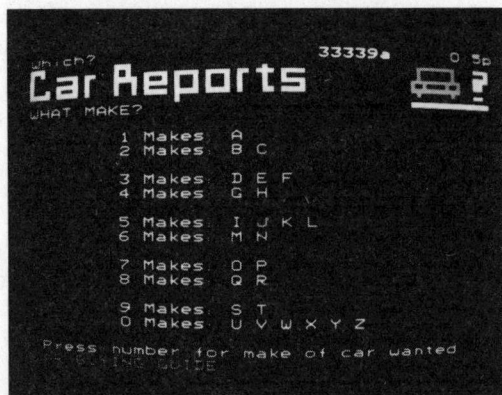
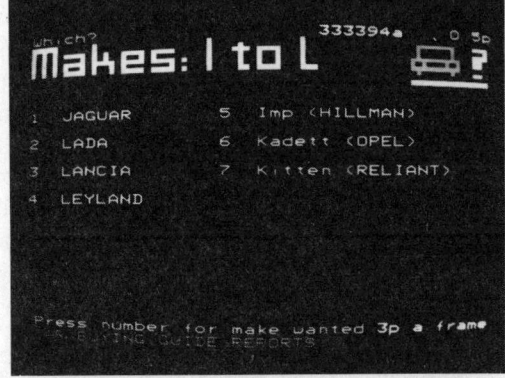
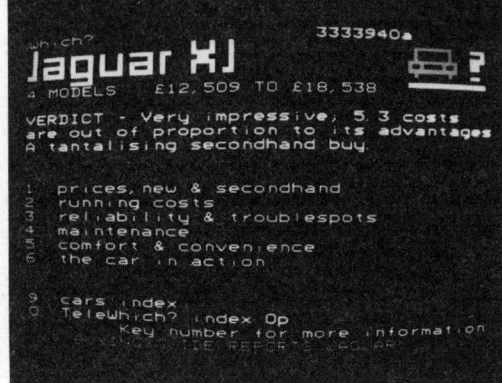

Serendipity is not simply a function of the choices available, it has much to do with the psyche, the mood, the interests, the time available and the pocket, the last being particularly important when it comes to the question of. 'What are we going to do?'

Now Viewdata differs from other media in a particularly subtle sense. It can allow for immensely rapid access to differing scales of windows on the world, from the broadest — the starting index level previously described in this chapter — to the narrowest — the single item specific.

In each case there is a sharp cut-off. The Viewdata world in which serendipity can occur is not one in which peripheral vision and the associated input play a large role. Unlike a printed magazine or journal, where much of the content can be gleaned at a glance, Viewdata presents a much narrower view. The characteristic of interest is that the user sets the width of the frame himself, and is not dependent upon externally derived arrangements. In some respects, Viewdata can be likened to operating a motion picture camera with zoom lens constantly changing the view in frame, the key difference being that with Viewdata the results are almost immediately apparent. (In an interesting parallel, this is also happening in the world of picture recording: video recorders with built-in cameras and instant picture are appearing just at the time that Viewdata comes to market.)

All this is a necessary preamble to considering the question, 'What are we going to do?'.

The evening out begins at the index page 0, the broadest of frames. Choice 1 gives access to the general subject of entertainment, further expanded in page 1 and finally in choice 3 of that page, page 13. At every step new possibilities will appear. The vista of seeming infinite choice may appear enticing, yet there is an underlying order, a structure.

Entertainment at page 13 covers the usual range of activities: cinemas, theatres, TV, radio, shows, musical events, festivals, night clubs, dancing, etc., on to eating out, sports and hobbies, jokes, quizzes and stories — a varied spectrum but

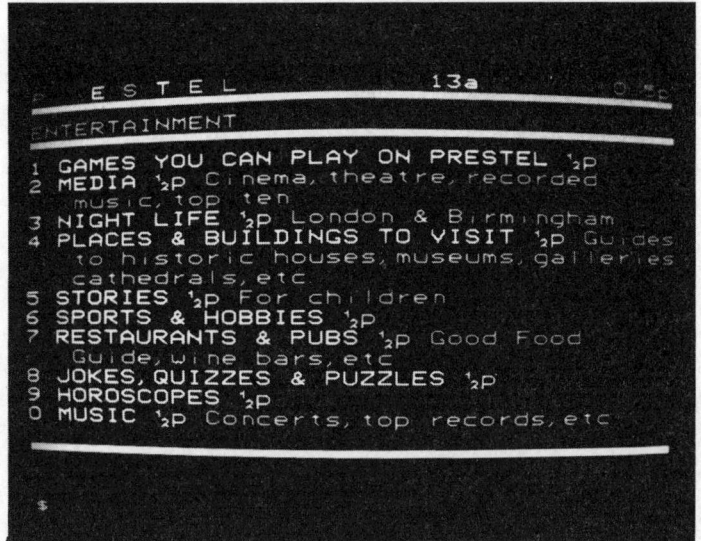

not one which is fixed. It can expand or contract as events and fashions change.

An evening out may well begin with the theatre, the cinema or a show. They are all explored from the gateway of page 13.

If one is seeking cinemas or theatres choice 2 calls the filial page 131 and the next page 1311 for cinemas, finally narrowing the selection to London at 1, Birmingham at 2 or Norwich at 3.* At this stage the viewer enters the gateway to the information source proper, the Information Provider.

In London *Time Out* provides 'The Movies', in Birmingham the *Birmingham Post and Mail* present the 'City Centre Cinemas' while in Norwich Eastel presents 'Cinemas and Theatres in Norwich and the Norfolk Area'.

Given that the evening out is in Norwich, go to page 408041. This will show a selection of places with details which can be obtained on keying the corresponding number 0-8.

But perhaps there's nothing on you wish to see? Return to page 13. Page 133, the next filial, covers night-clubs, dancing, discos, etc.

---

* UK market trial version.

Here as before there is a choice of locations. Again Birmingham is at choice 1, Norwich at 2, London at 3. 'Going out' in the Norwich area is the entry point. If eating and drinking is the choice, the next page (key 2) is the entry point to restaurants in the Norwich area. On choosing 'The Lansdowne' a full presentation on the first page, with a menu selection on the continuation page, is given.

Finding a suitable hotel in Norwich is a good illustration of the versatility and flexibility of the alphabetical search associated with the treeing method. On entry to the top index (page 0) choice 3 gives access to the alphabetical subject directory (page 199) from which with successive choice of 1, then 1 again, finally displays the directory section. This contains the word 'accommodation' and the corresponding page number, 1423, is the gateway to the subject.

Once the gateway number has been found, access to it is obtained by keying *1423#, the accommodation page from which 'hotels' are selected from amongst guest houses, camping and caravans; by keying choice 1; then the Information Provider, Eastel, who provide East Anglian information, from amongst a list of other Information Providers (the English Tourist Board, Centre Hotels and *Birmingham Post and Mail*) by keying 4; then the Norwich area, by keying 0.

A critical reader might comment that the procedure outlined so far is unnecessarily complicated; that the directory should not give the page number of the gateway to the accommodation page, but a direct jump to it by keying a single digit, as indeed is the case with much of the Viewdata procedures. It is possible to do this since fewer than ten choices are available on this particular directory page; indeed arrangements could be made that the maximum number of choices should be restricted to ten in all directory pages to simplify the search procedure and save time.*

A further selection from the range of room prices on offer

---

* One of the authors believes that the approach of the ten-by-ten matrix, if it could be imposed, would be a very good one. In this approach, the user would know that whatever function or facility was provided, there would be no more than ten possibilities. However, in the UK it is probably too late to impose this.

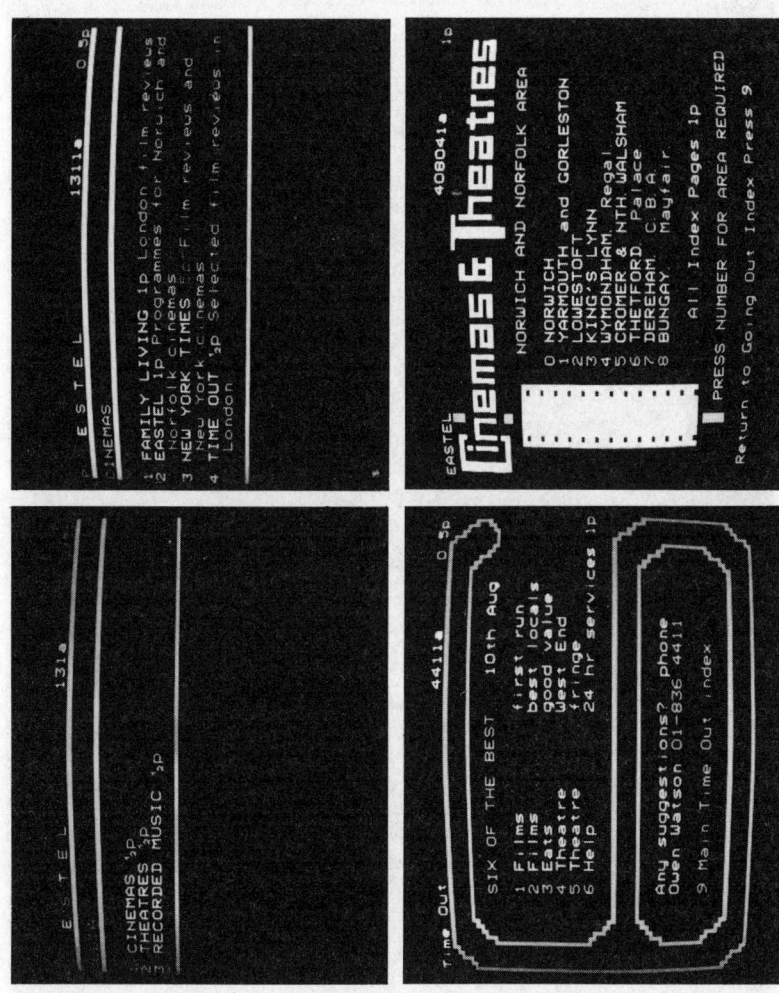

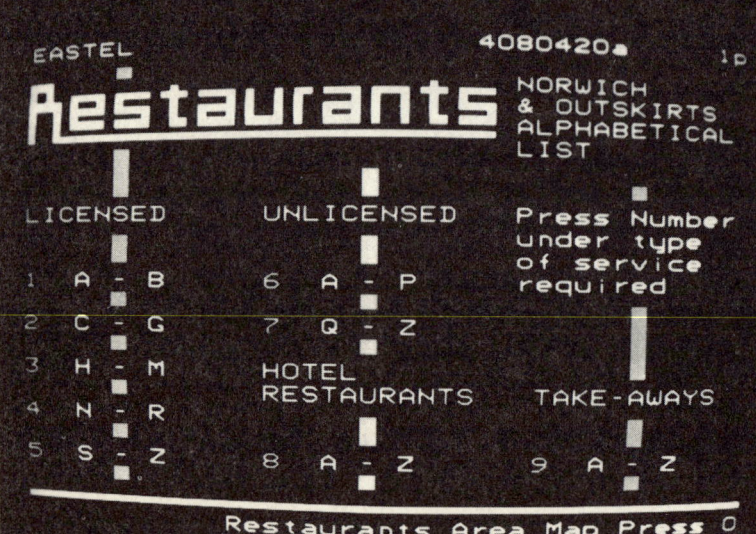

Information retrieval

(from under £4 to over £12 — 1978 prices!) finally gives access to an actual list of recommended hotels. The Castle Hotel — choice 4 — provides hard information; first, brief details, numbers of rooms, air conditioning etc., then the restaurant menu and the wine list in the continuation pages.

Conclusion

Clearly, more — or less — information could be made available. Whether it is to be more or less, the proper balance will eventually emerge. That balance will not satisfy everybody, but it will be the median, arrived at as a result of testing the market.

This median may bear little or no relationship to the amount of information that the information providers are now putting up. For the information currently being provided is a transfer from existing media both in form and content, and guided by reference to experience with those. A new medium however does not necessarily become a substitute — more likely it is an addition, as past experience has shown. Hence it carves its own niche, but the form in which that niche is carved we can as yet only guess at. We have ideas, we have convictions: but we could be wrong — and so could the information providers.

This possibility is not a view confined to the authors. Indeed a common analogy now in wide use looks at Prestel Viewdata services as if at a first-generation railway system in which the carriages look like horse-drawn coaches, the techniques and design expertise of the people and industry which built them coming necessarily from that prior industry.

But what was the prior industry? As we have shown, Viewdata technology is created from a mix of existing media technologies. A medium is not just a means of capturing information but also the transmission inherent within it. In carving out its own niche we can expect Viewdata, *pace* McLuhan, to invade existing media territory. A major territory likely to feel the impact is that of the mail, for with Viewdata technology mass market electronic mail could become economically viable — and thus profitable.

3 Electronic mail

The last chapter dealt primarily with the basis of a technology being actively brought to market in the UK, in which a triad of organisations otherwise acting independently have come together. What is being brought to the market can therefore be looked at in some detail. Electronic mail using Viewdata, however, deals with a group of like services, more dependent on the pace set by one organisation, and services moreover at a much earlier stage of development. What is being brought to market, and when, is not nearly so firmly fixed.

This chapter particularly is full of ironies, and we begin with one. It is the *new* Viewdata services which are coming to market first. By contrast, electronic mail — that is the transmission of messages by the use of electric wave forms — which comes to market later, is not new. Indeed, before electricity was discovered, the transmission of messages by optical means was commonplace: the first recorded proposal for a visual telegraph was made by the English physicist and chemist Robert Hooke in an address to the Royal Society in 1684. In 1790, the French engineer Claude Chappe introduced a network of semaphore stations in France which by 1852 had grown to 556 stations covering a total distance of 4820 kilometres.

The first proposal for replacing the visual with an electric telegraph was made in 1753 in Britain, but it was many years later after much experimentation that success was achieved, when the first commercial electric telegraph was installed for the Great Western Railway (by Cooke and Wheatstone) between Paddington and West Drayton in 1839, and extended to Slough in 1843. In 1845 it dramatically established its value to the layman when the operator at Paddington received a telegram from Slough informing him that a murder had been committed, that the suspect had boarded the 7.42 train to Paddington and had taken a seat in the last compartment of the second first-class carriage. The suspect was arrested on arrival, thus proving that the electric telegraph was faster than the fastest railway, and making the telegraph the talk of London.

The electric telegraph developed rapidly throughout Europe and the United States in the nineteenth and twentieth centuries, but it and its modern equivalent, the Telex service, remained essentially a tool for the businessman, to be used for special purposes, leaving the bulk of communications needs to be met by the physical transportation of written documents, by post or by verbal communication using the telephone.

So, given this background, how can Viewdata play a role in electronic mail? The answer is to be found in the economic circumstances which are bringing Viewdata to the market, and in the communications network technology of mass-market Viewdata.

The rationale underlying the pace at which Viewdata, in its information retrieval role, is being brought to that market was discussed in Chapter 1. A similar (though not an exact fit) rationale also applies to Viewdata as a system for electronic mail. The point to remember is that Viewdata is a, possibly *the,* system which unlocks the door to realising the economic potential lying within the home television receiver, but only if the information-provision handling structure and the communications networks to tie the receivers and the information system have been appropriately tailored.

If these exist, the normal mechanics of free enterprise, a better, i.e., a newer — with more facilities — mousetrap can be made to operate, at least at the terminal end. Generation 1 Viewdata receivers with a forty-character set, simple numeric pads with control buttons, can be succeeded by Generation 2 which could have a small built-in printer, and local tape cassette storage. Generation 3 could include a full alphanumeric keyboard; Generation 4 might go to a 2000-character screen and eighty characters to the line, the standard business correspondence width. No doubt there are other future variants of which we have no knowledge as yet. Hence though the initial Viewdata receiver has some limitations in an electronic mail role — for instance it would be useful to have some form of printer or reproduction-on-to-paper device — we can expect that those limitations will disappear with time as economic forces take their course.

Similar considerations apply when one considers the network technology: the initial network may not be the optimum for electronic mail applications. However, electronic mail possibilities are built into the starting network, even the more complex being inherent in the initial structure. Again, the growth of the market and usage of Viewdata is expected to drive the network in a direction which makes more complex, large-volume, long-message electronic mail not only possible but also easy to use — a necessity if mass-market electronic mail is to come about.

To understand why this should be so, we need to consider how Viewdata receivers, wherever they may be, are interconnected. This is shown in schematic form in Figure 3.1.

Consider the two Viewdata receivers located at A and B. It is the intention of the user at A to send a message to B.

User A keys in his message. As he does so, the characters are sent one at a time to the computer, CA, where they are stored. They are also immediately echoed back to the initiator's Viewdata screen at A so that it can be seen that the message transmitted is being received as sent, and without corruption.

Once the completed message has been stored in computer CA, it is automatically transmitted via the nearest local computer, computer CB, to Viewdata receiver B.

But how does computer CA *connect* with computer CB? This is accomplished by a dedicated telecommunications line linking the two. That dedicated link is one of many between

52   Viewdata revolution

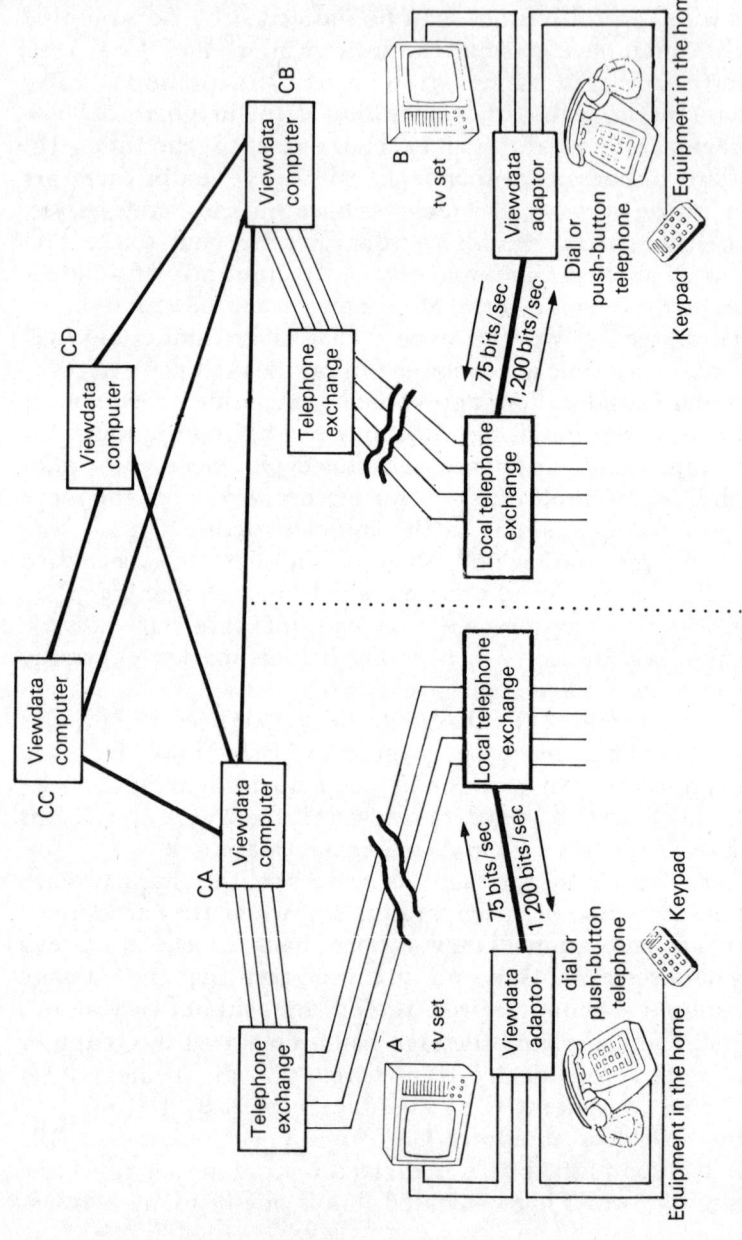

Figure 3.1   Schematic diagram of Viewdata network

Electronic mail 53

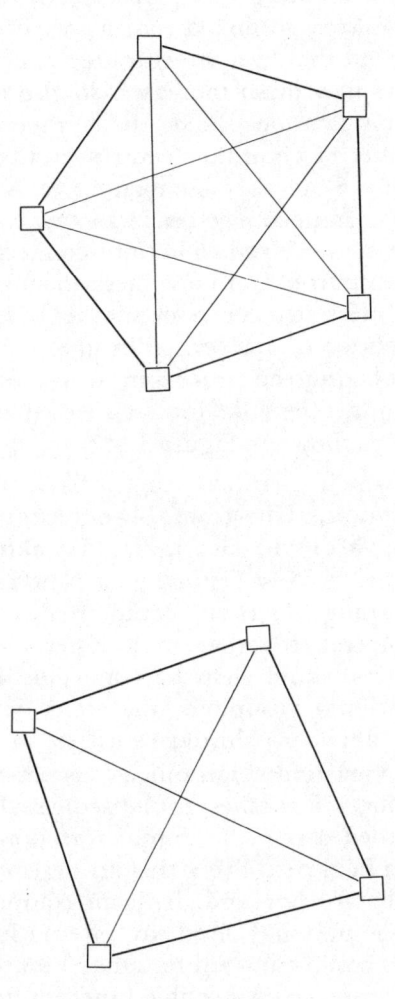

Number of interconnections with a mesh of 4 centres is 6

Number of interconnections with a mesh of 5 centres is 10

Figure 3.2 In a mesh of computer centres every computer is connected to every other one, so that if one adds a computer to an existing mesh of say four centres, the number of computer connections increases by 4, instead of just by one (the general formula is n(n + 1))

the Viewdata computers: for CA and CB are part of a mesh of computer centres interconnected for message communications.

Figure 3.1 shows such a mesh. It consists of four interconnected computer centres, so linked that messages can flow from any one centre to another by a direct route.

As the number of centres in a mesh increases, so also does the number of intercommunications links. It is therefore necessary to keep the number of computer centres in a mesh down to a reasonably small (5—6) number (see Figure 3.2). Additional computer centres will be grouped together in another mesh, and so on. Obviously these meshes need to be interconnected, so that messages may be transmitted from one mesh to another and from one centre in one mesh to a centre in another. This is best arranged by the nomination of one computer in one mesh as the junction station, repeating the process in all the other meshes. Junction stations may then be interconnected in a separate mesh of their own, as shown in Figure 3.3.

In a large urban area in which Viewdata usage is likely to be heavy; for example London, Glasgow, Manchester or Birmingham in the UK; Munich, Stuttgart, Frankfurt, Cologne, Dusseldorf, Hamburg in West Germany; or New York, Boston, Philadelphia, Washington; there could in time be several local meshes, connected together in a super mesh. The super meshes themselves would then be connected into even larger regional or national groupings, maintaining the principle of connection between similar entities at all levels. Thus the 'national' Viewdata communications network is a hierarchical connection of meshes each dedicated to Viewdata, themselves formed from the interconnection of existing telecommunication facilities. Using this arrangement, it is possible to go one step further and dedicate computer centres at the regional or national level to international Viewdata communications, connecting up national Viewdata systems as they come into existence. A possible (and currently likely) international mesh based on this network architecture is shown in Figure 3.4.

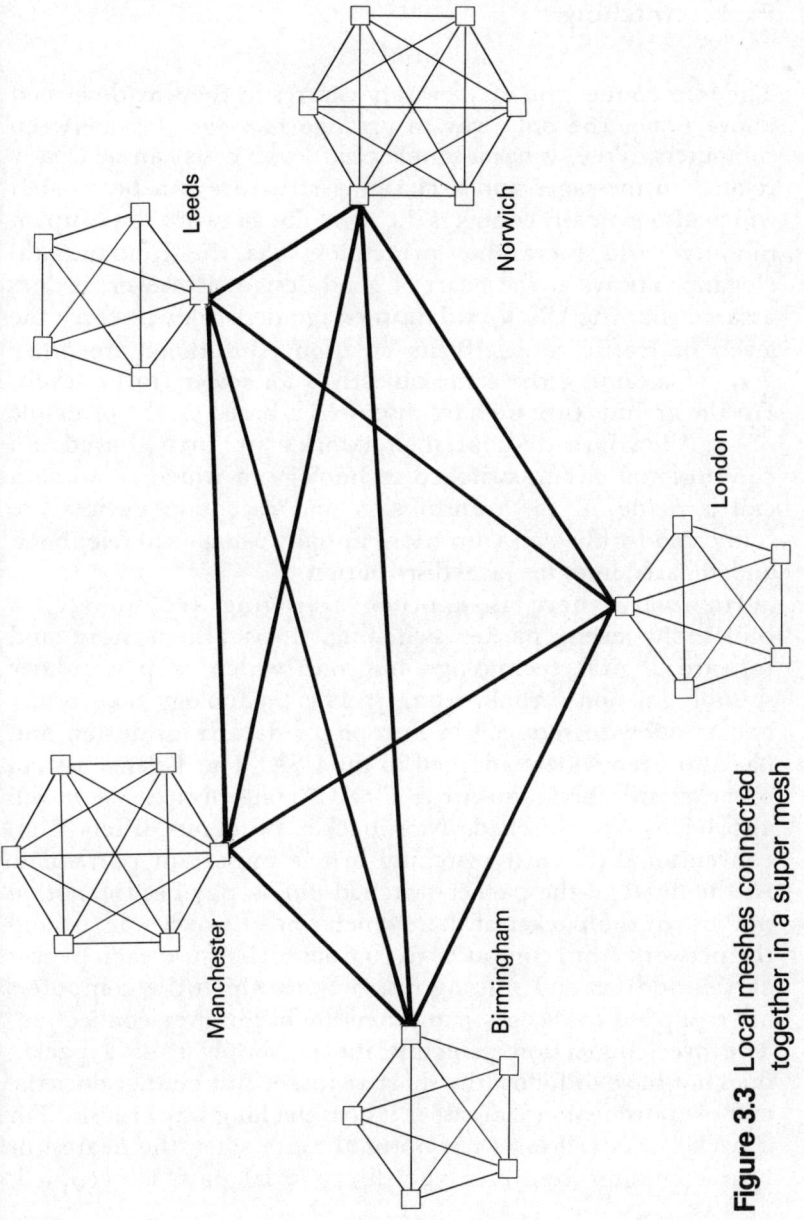

Figure 3.3 Local meshes connected together in a super mesh

Packet switching

The interconnection of Viewdata centres in the way described above is not the only way to arrange message flow between computers. True, it has a simple clear logic: costs can be clearly related to messages and a charging structure can be created which also logically connects the two. The network, built up on modular and hierarchic principles, has the fundamental elegance always at the heart of good design. However, it does assume that the UK Viewdata message network will carry the levels of traffic to justify its creation. But there are other ways of attaining the same objectives for lower traffic levels. For the architecture we have discussed is based on the principle of a Viewdata-dedicated network, in turn based on conventional circuit-switched technology in which — when a call is made — the transmission and reception devices are connected for the call's duration, initially using local telephone undedicated lines for local distribution.

However, there is another switching technology, a philosophy even: packet switching. It is also a store and forward digital technology but one which is particularly suitable for non-verbal messages. This technology is currently being widely introduced in Europe for data transmission and has also been widely adopted in the USA. The Telenet system is packet-switched, and AT & T's ACS transmission system will also be packet switched. Now packet switching differs from conventional (circuit) switching in one important particular. At the heart of the packet-switched philosophy lies the notion not just of the packet of data which finds its own way around the network from computer to computer (because each packet carries address and routing instructions which the computers are equipped to recognise and handle) but of over-connection. The over-connection principle means simply this: a packet does not have to follow the shortest route. But neither does the cost of transmission increase if it goes the long way around. For a packet only follows a not-optimal route when the nearest or next computer centre in the direct serial path is occupied.

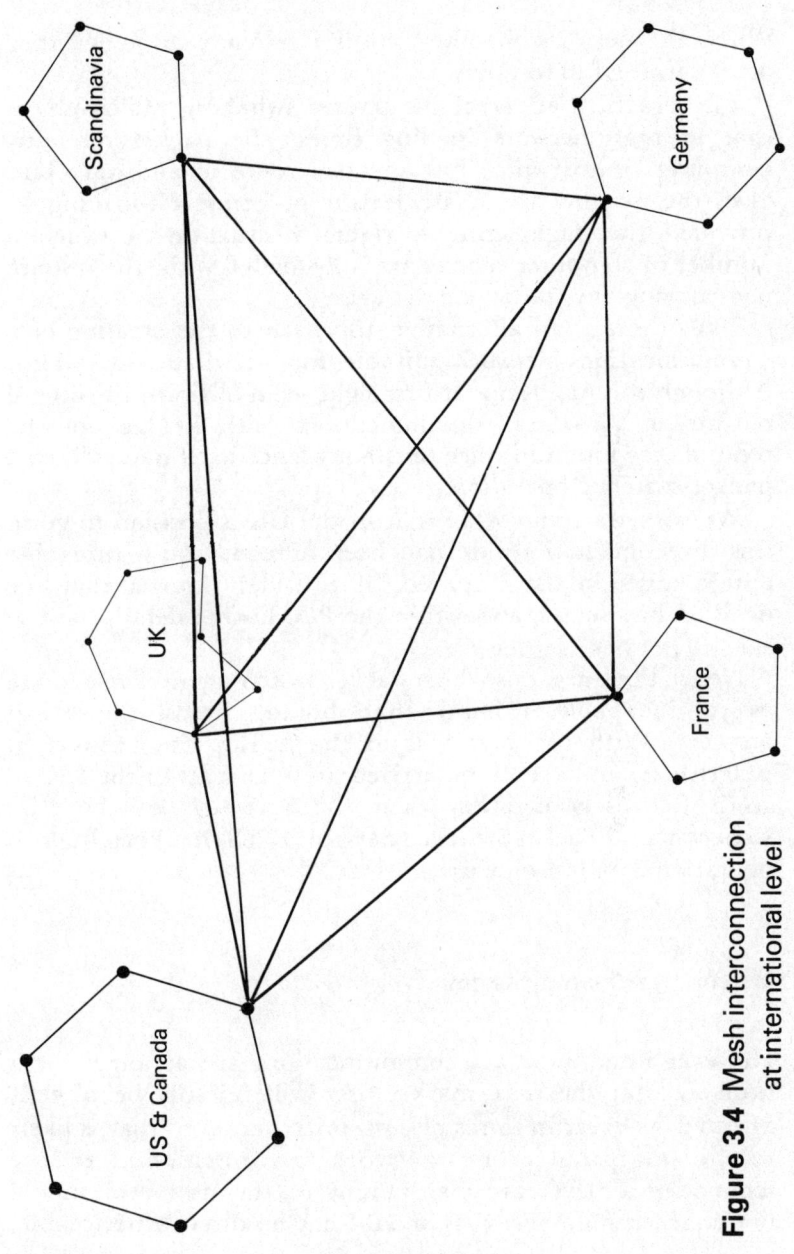

Figure 3.4 Mesh interconnection at international level

When the network in other words is already at some other point earning full revenues.

The practical effect of the packet switching philosophy is that at high network loading times, the packets use any computer centre which has an open route in and out. This gives the network the characteristic of being self-loading — provided the engineering is right, a situation in which a number of computer centres are fully loaded while the rest are not carrying any traffic, cannot arise.

Thus there is an alternative approach to the creation of a communications network suitable for Viewdata operations. Although this might not at first sight seem obvious, the digital nature of Viewdata communications with its lack of the redundancy found in voice telephony lends itself naturally to a packet-switched operation.

We wish we could write that in the UK a decision to go in this direction nationwide had been agreed, and a timetable and detailed plans prepared. It is widely known that the decision has been made within the PO, but no details have so far still not been settled.

Hence the questions which packet switching gives rise to are as yet incapable of more than broad, almost theoretical answers. With the best will in the world, the answers in practice are unlikely to be arrived at — at least in the UK — until the early eighties when the successor to the PO's Experimental Packet Switched Service (EPSS) has been built, is operational and in wide use.

Person to person messages

However inter-Viewdata communications are arranged, it is unlikely that the mass-market user will initially be directly affected — exect in terms of cost/price and even that is likely to be marginal. The network arrangements at the technological level are transparent to the user and should not concern him/her: they should not be directly noticeable.

They are of import to businesses which intend to devise compatible networks of their own, or where equipment has to be bought. But the network is probably the last facility that the user as user is concerned with. Much more important to him or her is what is seen and handled directly, and communication at this level is more concerned with 'How do I actually go about sending a message?' and 'What is the rationale which guides the action: why are the facilities built in one particular way and not another, so that I can do *this*, but not *that*?

The starting point of the Prestel-Viewdata message service when considered in this way is to be found in the principles which guided Viewdata's creation: simplicity and a close attention to practical psychology, attempting within the limitations of the technology to simulate in Viewdata normal methods of message handling with which ordinary people are not only familiar, but are accustomed to using daily and almost instinctively and quite effectively.

As the technology exists in the late seventies, it is not possible to communicate with a computer system in a free-form natural language, using phrases in a message environment of the kind, 'Please take a message to so and so'. Instead, different conventions are used, and on accessing the Prestel-Viewdata message service the system initiates the conversation. This is a quite normal standard technique in good computer dialogue design, closely analogous to that used in human communications in situations where a person approaches an organisation which hopes to sell him/her something; airlines, hotels, shops and the like, a service relationship. What is critical to such a dialogue is that the party being addressed, in this case the computer, seems to initiate the substantive conversation.

So how would (or does, because it has been working on the British Post Office's own experimental system) a message system work? On switching on and dialling up the Prestel-Viewdata service, the system responds by identifying itself, showing that it is Prestel-Viewdata, and indicating the last time that it was used by the caller. Then follow the standard instructions to use the keypad and go to the next page: the

Index page showing the choice of services available. Currently message services are choice 8*. When you key 8, the next page displayed will offer the choice of alternative message services such as television representations of greetings cards, or instant messages for commuters.* Several options are possible within the greetings card service: 'Happy Birthday' and 'Happy Anniversary' being obvious examples.

Prestel Viewdata show a typical if rather more than usually stylised Christmas card. Also at the top of the frame there now appears a pair of red flashing stars, to draw attention to a caption which reads 'To user', and a 'prompt' at the bottom of the frame stating, 'Please enter destination user number'. This is the equivalent of the recipient's address, and the number may be a phone number, or a separate user number if the phone number is insufficient for identification. The user now keys the recipient's address number. The system will in turn check the number in its list against names, identify the recipient and put up his name. The prompt now changes to read, 'Please key # to send message.' This enables the user to amend the message if part has been keyed-in in error.

But how does the user go about selecting a greetings card representation and transmitting it? Take 'Merry Christmas'.

First, key 8 for message service, which will bring up page 8. Now go to choice 1 on that page to select the greetings card service. This will bring up page 81 which will show that choice 9 is 'Merry Christmas'. Press 9 and page 819 now appears.

You will note that the paging once again — as in the information retrieval service — follows a logical sequence, one convention that the page number is displayed at the top right-hand corner of the frame is followed here also.) This is a powerful reinforcement tool, as once the user understands how he reached it he can follow the logic through in other services. It can also provide a simple short cut throughout the system: as

---

* An early version of the commuter message service which caused much amusement during the early demonstrations of Viewdata in 1975/76 is shown on p. 72. Choice 3 — devised by Brian Knott, a major influence on the construction of an intelligent and friendly dialogue — usually brought the largest laugh.

in information retrieval with Prestel-Viewdata, the user can key in page 819 and go to it directly.

Suppose that the message as entered is correct and the prompted transmission key is pressed, the prompt now changes to 'Message despatched'. At the same time the system shows, at the top of the frame, the date and time at which the message was transmitted, followed by the words 'sent on'.

However, it does not follow that a message once sent through Viewdata has necessarily been received. This depends on the message receiving option in the recipient's receiver. The simplest option is that in which Prestel-Viewdata will tell the would-be recipient that a message awaits him but only when he switches the receiver on and connects up to Prestel-Viewdata. This is shown on the welcome page which greets the user when identified by the system. Underneath the user number, it will state:

'There is a new message waiting for you.'
'Please key *80☐ to receive messages.'

This done, the message is displayed; it is identical to the one sent except that it now shows the name/user number of the initiator.

A number of facilities already exist which allow us to go beyond the simple routine so far outlined, and others are under development.

One of the most useful is probably the 'flash on the screen' displayed by Prestel-Viewdata if the user happens to be connected, but not active. As soon as a message is received by the local computer it, finding that the recipient is already connected, immediately sends a line now displayed at the bottom of the screen which reads:

'Message for you just received. Please key *80☐.'

(Alternatively this prompt may be displayed when the user next calls for another page.)

If however the person for whom the message is intended is not connected at the time, then the local computer can dial the telephone number automatically. When the telephone handset is picked up a high-pitched tone is heard; this is the Viewdata computer 'signature tune', indicating that the computer is calling. To receive the message, it is simply necessary to switch on the Viewdata receiver and push the button marked Prestel on the keypad, when the identifier frame will be displayed and will indicate that a new message is waiting.

The next facility to be considered deals with the situation where nobody answers the telephone when the computer dials. Here the automatic answering device attached — or built in to the Viewdata receiver comes into its own. When the computer calls, the automatic answering unit simulates the lifting of the telephone handset and, recognising the high-pitched tone sent by the computer, sends back an acknowledgement tone, followed by the user number and the password. It then switches on its internal audio cassette recorder and accepts a recording of the message. When the user returns to his telephone he can play back the message from the cassette recorder to the Viewdata receiver. (It is immediately apparent that this system cannot work unless cassette recorders are built in to Viewdata receivers — our possible second-generation receiver).

The user number is a temporary expedient: it has been replaced by an identification number sent by the Viewdata receiver automatically to the computer at connect time, as soon as the high-pitched tone has been identified. A password may be required but only where a higher degree of security is demanded by the user. Generally this is not needed, and the identification number sent out by the terminal identifies the installation rather than the user himself in the same way that a telephone number identifies the telephone instrument rather than the person answering the telephone. However, while in the latter case it is not possible to add a personal identification, with Viewdata this requirement is met quite easily by adding a password. Indeed, more than one password can be added if a higher degree of security is required.

If the Viewdata receiver identification is sent automatically by the receiver, how will messages be addressed to other Viewdata users? The answer is of course to associate Viewdata users with their telephone numbers. Instead of entering the user number of a Viewdata subscriber one would enter his telephone number, which could be obtained from the telephone directory. The installation number, sent out automatically by the Viewdata receiver at connect time, could also be the telephone number.

There are advantages in using a person's telephone number as his Viewdata address. The major one is that the local Viewdata computer (which accepts your message for transmission to another user) is enabled to identify easily the remote computer centre to which the message has to be relayed before it can be sent on to the addressee.

Once the message has arrived at the remote centre all further work is done by that centre. It may, for instance, be required to call the user several times to ensure that the message is actually delivered to the person for whom it is intended rather than deposited in a tape recorder. The message may be private and a password may need to be checked before the message is delivered. If an acknowledgement is required this also has to be done by the remote centre.

The message facility is clearly very powerful. It means you could send a message to anybody who is on Viewdata with the surety of delivery, and with the possibility of confirmation where required. In this mode Viewdata can also specify whether the message has been deposited in a tape recorder or whether it was delivered to the person for whom it was intended. One particularly interesting aspect of the message service is the ability to send a message to somebody who may not be accessible on the telephone at the time one needs to get in touch with them. (Commuters must be particularly conscious of the dilemma they often find themselves in when, not infrequently, they need to telephone home so as to get somebody to meet them at the station, and the phone number is engaged or there is no-one yet there to reply.)

Abuses of message service?

But if it is so easy to use Viewdata for message transfer, can it be abused? The answer must be 'yes' in the sense that every power and every capability can *and will* be abused by somebody. The telephone can be abused: you may be called out of bed in the middle of the night by somebody with a peculiar sense of humour. Obscene, rude or simply insulting calls on the telephone are not uncommon. The police and the fire service get large numbers of hoax telephone messages in almost all countries. The situation then is not new, but with Viewdata the hoaxer can be identified. He has to give his personal identity number before his message can be accepted by the system, and because of this the likelihood of abuse is much reduced. Of course, the familiar hoax/obscene call problem may well arise once more when Viewdata sets become publicly accessible — just like public phone boxes: already, coin-operated Prestel receivers have been installed at some large stores and hotels in London, but the identity of the originating receiver is automatically recorded, and therefore abuse is far less likely.

Another abuse of the telephone, which is probably also to be expected with Viewdata, is the advertising call. The advertiser calls to tell you about the wonders of brand X, just when you must dash out. Mail shots of advertisers can be even more irritating, particularly when you get shoals of written matter when you are looking for an important letter which has not arrived. With Viewdata technology this kind of thing is very easy. For example, the same message can be repeated to a lot of people as long as they are on Viewdata, by simply using the multiple-address facility. This means that when you have finished entering the message on Viewdata it asks for any other addresses to which you wish to have the message repeated. Thereafter the computer does all the work, calling each address individually and delivering the message. With Viewdata, this abuse can be easily prevented, since the Viewdata-operating authority can withdraw the facility from those who abuse it.* This is unlike the situation with ordinary mail, where the envelope containing the advertising matter may not carry any identification.

A major difference between ordinary written messages and those carried by Viewdata is that the former arrive on a piece of paper, and can therefore be kept indefinitely, while the latter can only be observed on the television screen, and at that in practice only for a short while. Because of this a number of additional facilities are being introduced on Viewdata.

There is first the now ubiquitous audio-cassette recorder, which may be plugged into a specially provided socket in the Viewdata receiver to take a record of any Viewdata frame desired. Already in some Viewdata receivers you only have to press the button marked 'record' after you have switched the cassette recorder on. (In some other receivers you have to key *00, getting the computer to repeat the current frame being displayed.) If the cassette recorder has been previously switched on, set of course to record, then a recording of the repeated frame will be taken as it is transmitted. The frame recorded may now be played back (while the receiver is still connected or on-line) by switching the recorder to 'playback'. The button on the keypad (marked 'phone hold') will hold the telephone line while the playback takes place. This enables the user to take a recording of several pages, and check them all with the minimum of time delay, without incurring the risk of finding the line engaged once the connection has been broken.

Although the cassette recorder was devised to take sound recordings, this is sufficient to record the image on the television receiver, including Viewdata's colours and graphics. This is because the cassette recorder takes a record of the *sounds* transmitted down the telephone line: the same sounds which were used to create the Viewdata picture. During playback these sounds are applied to the Viewdata-adapted television set and consequently reproduce the intended message.

---

* There is a precedent in the reactions to (and possible legislation against) the automatic phone dialler in the USA.

In many cases the cassette recorder is clearly not the ideal storage device. If the message is to be shown to somebody who has not got a Viewdata-adapted television receiver, sending him a cassette will not solve the problem. What is needed is a photograph or other copy of the message on paper (with or without colour, though preferably with). One obvious way of arranging this is to take a photo of the screen with an instant reproduction camera, and Viewdata receivers with this attachment will no doubt become available when the public service gets under way.

However, the instant camera is clearly not the answer when it comes to taking more than the occasional copy of a Viewdata message. Initially, business users — because the service will not at the beginning be as cheap as one would like — can expect to use Viewdata receivers fitted with hard-copy printer units of the matrix type. These printers are so designed that characters are built up of a matrix of points and only the appropriate points are inked-in to show the profile of the character. (Indeed this is the way characters are displayed on the screen but the characters are so small that the individual dots are virtually indistinguishable.) They could be manufactured quite cheaply if the volumes are high — and we expect this to happen within one or two years.

Ordinary alphabetic characters are usually made up with a matrix of 5×7 dots. Figure 3.5 shows the letter A displayed as a matrix of dots. The letter B following the A shows the spacing between the two — sometimes one dot, sometimes two, depending on the make of receiver. A descending character, such as g in lower case, needs more dots below the line so that altogether each character space needs a minimum matrix of 6×10 to be capable of coping with all the shapes likely to be encountered in Viewdata. In practice a matrix of 12×20 is used on large-size Viewdata receivers to provide character 'rounding' and thus a more pleasing display.

A matrix printer providing all the facilities described is called an area printer, since every inch of the total hard copy area of the paper may be covered. Hence these are very suitable for Viewdata, as they are capable of copying not only

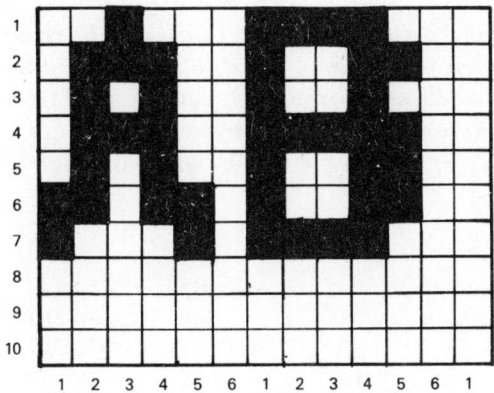

5 × 7 Dot matrix for alphabetic characters

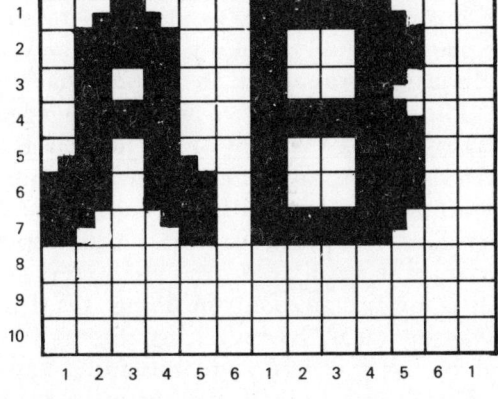

5 × 7 Dot matrix with character rounding

Figure 3.5

alphabetic and numeric characters but also the whole range of graphic characters (such as those which are used to make up a picture similar to that on any graphical frame).

The matrix printer is not, however, really suitable for the office. A business letter is now usually typed to a high typographic standard and this practice is unlikely to die out because of Viewdata. However, Viewdata-modified electric typewriters are expected to become available, so that the hard copy resulting from a Viewdata message can look as freshly typed as that from current machines. (However, with current technology the ability to display graphics and to reproduce colours would be lost.)

Viewdata business mail

As Viewdata can be readily used for the transmission of person-to-person messages, why not business mail? Indeed the discussion on hard-copy devices above had to refer to business mail because much of this kind of mail must have hard copy.

Leaving aside for the moment additional special features sometimes needed for business mail, how would it operate on Viewdata? In the first place it would probably not be economic to maintain a continuous link between the typist and the Viewdata computer. The typing speed of a fully engaged, experienced typist working from clear copy or instructions is of the order of 5-6 characters per second, roughly 50-60 words per minute. This is a very low speed compared with the capability of the telephone/Viewdata computer link and the display device. The computer may be made to accept characters at a much higher rate, but there is little point in doing this if the typist cannot take advantage of it. By preparing the mail off-line, the limitation of typing speed is overcome and a faster transmission speed from terminal to computer may be adopted. Apart from the poor economics of preparing business mail on-line, i.e. while being continually connected to the Viewdata computer, if the practice became widespread it could lead to extensive congestion of the telephone system, particularly in the switching plant. In order to avoid this, the obvious answer is to prepare the mail off-line, i.e. without actually being connected to the Viewdata computer. A special terminal is required for that, one rather similar to a word processor (though simpler, cheaper and easier to operate). In other words, the terminal needs to be 'intelligent'.

With current developments in low-cost, small-space microprocessors, which can provide a substantial amount of computer power, the provision of inexpensive adequate intelligence within the Viewdata terminal will soon become a reality. As the technology is now economically available, such terminals could be widely in operation in the UK in the early eighties. Assuming that development takes place at this rate it would then be possible for businesses to prepare much of their mail using a business Viewdata terminal. This would provide facilities for accepting letters typed on a keyboard and displayed on the television screen. Corrections, amendments, additions, deletions would be made on the screen using editing controls on the terminal. The new kind of business terminal would use the same kind of protocols as used on Viewdata, so that the same method of learning/operation of the system would obtain.

Continuing the Viewdata business-mail scenario, mail is prepared off-line on the terminal throughout the day and stored in it while being prepared. Urgent mail may be transmitted to the local computer as soon as ready, but non-urgent mail — i.e. mail which need not be delivered before the next morning — is left stored in the terminal. When the evening peak* viewing period is over the Viewdata computer is made to call each individual business terminal in turn, to check if any mail needs to be collected. If collection is required, it instructs the terminal to transmit this mail to it at high speed, together with any instructions regarding its delivery, i.e. multiple addressing, requests for acknowledgement, request for certification of delivery, delivery to a named individual or a legal proxy, etc. Clearly a number of security procedures will need to be developed to

---

* It is anticipated that three peak viewing periods on Viewdata will develop during weekdays in line with telephone usage patterns: the first two corresponding to the two peak periods of the telephone — mainly due to the two peaks of business activity — during the mid-morning and mid-afternoon, and the third, the domestic, using home Viewdata in the evening, possibly giving a peak usage at about 6 or 7 o'clock in single set homes, and probably later in those with more than one.

ensure that as far as possible abuse is prevented. Some indeed are already on the way to being implemented.

Each Viewdata computer collects mail from all business terminals within its area and stores it locally. The mail is then segregated or sorted automatically according to the remote Viewdata computer to which it is to be despatched for distribution in that computer's local area. Then follows the exchange of mail between computers, using the intra-computer network described earlier. Finally Viewdata computers deliver the mail to its ultimate destination, this being done according to a similar procedure used for collecting mail. The Viewdata computer calls the required business terminal automatically. The terminal is programmed to answer the call and to identify itself automatically by sending a prearranged code, which if necessary may be encyphered (encrypted). On completion of the identification procedure, the Viewdata computer transmits the total mail addressed to the particular terminal, collects acknowledgements, certificates of delivery etc., and goes on to service the next terminal.

Though some of the experimental design work has been done in the UK, programs do not as yet exist on Prestel to implement these functions in their entirety or with the necessary degree of efficiency. However, the design and implementation of the software required should not pose great difficulties.

Assuming all this is done, what is the benefit to the business? The benefit is not only economic, but also in many ways results in a higher-quality service than can be provided by the physical transportation of the written word. Urgent mail, for example, may be sent instantly and replies received equally quickly. Mail may be sent and received at any time depending on the exigencies of the business. Viewdata is a twenty-four-hours-a-day, seven-days-a-week service, without a break throughout the year. This particular attribute is probably of more value to the individual who, unlike the businessman, has very limited financial resources to fall back on in times of emergency (outside the kind of emergency which modern society is prepared to accept as worthy of some assistance such

as a large-scale catastrophe involving the many, etc.).
What of the economic benefit? Taking current UK charges for telephone calls and making very conservative assumptions about the cost of running and equipping Viewdata centres, it is estimated roughly that the price of collecting, transmitting and delivering an A4-size page (at 1978 cost/inflation levels) should be no more than about 4p (USA 8 cents). This compares with about 20p per letter (excluding typing and editing) which is the current — 1978 — cost of handling a letter in a UK organisation. The price of 4p per A4 page applies to the long-distance traffic, since the short-distance traffic, particularly local mail, is considerably cheaper to handle. Even then a very important factor has been deliberately omitted from the equation; business mail on Prestel could be carried at marginal costing, i.e. for almost nothing, since all costs could be recouped on the main Prestel-Viewdata operations during the busy hours when using information retrieval and other facilities. Alternatively, the extension of Viewdata to the handling of business mail could, by sharing the cost between all services, result in a much cheaper service to the customer, whether daytime or night-time. This factor in turn should result in a larger customer base, and in producing the effects of the 'virtuous circle' with the systems costs stabilising at a lower value even than those indicated.

A fairly fundamental assumption has been made early on regarding the preparation of mail off-line. The assumption is that such a mode of working is likely to be far more economic than the on-line mode, i.e. using a remote computer and the telephone network for accessing to it. The present cost of word processor systems does not fully justify this view. However it is likely that a well designed Viewdata system could provide a more economic word-processing service than some of the currently available dedicated machines.

Telex

A development of much more immediate impact on business mail would also be possible with Viewdata if the simple software already demonstrated were to be further developed and applied to augment and enhance the facilities of Telex. In the normal Viewdata system the Viewdata computers are accessible via the telephone network, but it is equally possible to provide access to the Prestel computers via the Telex network or indeed via both networks.

But what has Prestel-Viewdata to offer Telex? Essentially it provides three important enhancements. The first is the (so-called) store and foreward facility, which enables the Telex operator to deposit his message in the local Prestel-Viewdata computer and to rely on the latter to send it on to its destination via the Telex network: this is different from the present Telex situation where a connection must be established between the calling and called Telex machines before the message can be passed on.* While the current procedure may be acceptable when traffic is not heavy, it is time-consuming at peak hours. (The local Telex connection to the Prestel-Viewdata computer is not likely to suffer the same peak loading as it is possible to provide adequate local traffic-bearing circuits at relatively low cost, since these are essentially short distance circuits.)

The second Telex enhancement is the message-repeat facility. Once a message has been deposited in the Prestel-Viewdata computer, an instruction may be added to repeat it to several other destinations. This might apply to a notice calling numbers of people to a meeting, or one passing information required by several persons all at the same address (or at different addresses). At present it is usually necessary to establish a telex connection with each destination telex machine and to repeat the message every time the connection is made. The only way to avoid keying the same message to each destination is to first record it on paper tape and run the

---

* New Telex systems are now being installed to provide the store and forward capability.

tape on the machine once for each destination, and then only when each connection has been established.

The third enhancement is the ability to by-pass the telex room at certain times. It is well known that the telex system, like the telephone, has peak periods during which telex messages accumulate awaiting collection and distribution within the organisation served by that telex room: delays of up to one or more hours are not unknown. This is where Viewdata becomes very useful. Provided the intended recipient has a Viewdata receiver nearby, the telex message may be repeated to that Viewdata terminal by the local Viewdata computer (if the instruction to do so is given in the originating message). Little ingenuity would be required to make this instruction dependent on the state of the traffic at the distant end.

The enhancement of the telex network that can be brought about with Viewdata may well be extended world-wide to the international telex system. Naturally, it will be necessary for this extension to associate international Viewdata numbers to telex numbers and identify individual extensions on the local Viewdata computer. Such standardisation requires international agreement between PTTs, and will therefore take some time, but it is almost certain to come. The extensive and complex machinery of CCITT (Comité Consultatif International de Télégraphe et de Téléphone) has already begun to seek for consensus and agreement.

However, even this delay to the development of a numbering system suitable for Telex and Prestel may be mitigated in a very considerable way in large organisations by using an intelligent terminal in the telex room, particularly in those most likely to suffer from peak-hour congestion.

Personalised messages

One of the greatest objections to electronic mail is the impersonal nature of the message. Apart from characteristics embedded in the actual content, it is generally not possible visually to identify the sender. Indeed, where the content of the message is such that the sender is easily identified, usually because of some item of information which only one person is thought likely to be familiar with, the danger of false identification is greater, possibly because of the relative implausibility of an error. This is where handwriting has an enormous advantage over the typescript, and consequently a physical letter over the telegram.

Viewdata in its current form does not yet provide a sufficiently good screen resolution to allow for the display of a handwritten signature which would identify the sender as reliably as standard security devices (and most of those are currently too expensive for the mass market). Given this, what can then be done to personalise — and secure — Viewdata messages?

One improvement we expect to see introduced quite quickly is a greater resolution on the screen. Screen resolution is related to the amount of storage incorporated in the Viewdata receiver, and storage is a fairly cheap commodity, the cost of which has been falling steadily for some years (40 per cent per annum). The related improvement is to introduce a device similar to that developed by the Dutch called the Telewriter (created in a series of studies intended to introduce a low-cost system of education in Indonesia). Essentially this device consists of a tablet made up of two electrically conducting sheets so arranged that the pressure of a pencil on the top sheet causes an electrical contact between the two sheets at the point of contact. The tablet is connected to a control unit which alternately measures the resistance between the top edges of the sheets and between the side edges, thus determining the position of the pencil. This then is transmitted over the telephone line to the collaborating receiver and displayed on a television screen. With normal writing speeds the amount of information transmitted is so low that it can be superimposed on voice without any cross-interference. This sort of device is easily adaptable to Viewdata, and could provide a simple means of transmitting hand-written signatures for message identification.

However the best message service, and certainly the most secure (at least in the sense of ensuring that the recipient is in fact the person intended) comes from turning the act of one-way communication into a two-way conversation. In one sense of course, this is not new, and could obviously be done with a Telex-Viewdata linked service as previously discussed. The difference were Prestel-Viewdata to go in this direction would come from the mass-market nature of Prestel-Viewdata. There is considerable operational difference between a service relying on a one-company or one-organisation simple-terminal facility, and a service in which the terminals are linked to telephone extensions, with a number present on each floor or department.

The first one-terminal situation is remarkably similar to that which existed in organisations before the Xerox machine arrived. The pre-Xerox copying processes, with their stencil-typing requirements and the usual one-per-building location, were notorious paper production bottlenecks. The one-per-floor Xerox is not: indeed except for the production of large and bulky documents, reproduction schedules hardly exist any more: the xerox is just something you use when you need it.

The same sort of difference is expected to arise with Viewdata. Thus the distinction between the two stages is not simply quantitative but also qualitative.

Similar differences apply also in the home market, but here even more sharply. Qualitatively, the difference is between real-time and batch; between Prestel-Viewdata and a postal system which at best runs on a twenty-four-hour delivery basis. Quantitatively the difference is even more marked: it is between no real-time paper or written-word automatic-handling facility and the facility itself — there is no more marked difference than that.

So overall, if one looks at possible message services, the differences between pre- and post-Viewdata situations are quite sharp. They are not simply those of numbers and the resultant complexity or lack of it — they also stem from the nature and quality of the service that can be devised, and the usage patterns that might develop.

So how might Viewdata be developed to overcome the difference between no market and some? For it is obvious that the type of service initially introduced will be critical to the future development of Prestel-Viewdata, and will in turn determine in part the type of service to be offered thereafter. For the old rule that the initial set trajectory is a constraint on the outcome will apply to Viewdata as it does to any other technology.

The services (possible, probable, likely) we have so far discussed are of different types. The network technology will allow for many variants subsumed under the title 'electronic mail'; bulk mail transmission, individual one-shot mail, person-to-person messages, have different characteristics. The analogues for the first two are the postal and Telex systems as they exist, the analogue for the third is — partially — the greetings telegram service in which the message element is pre-set, leaving only the personal data — time of origin, destination, names — which will give it meaning, to be introduced.

A full conversational service however is different: it is free form, and the analogue for that is in fact the telephone system. This is fitting, because it is more dependent upon the telephone system than any of the others, with which the bulk of applications and users are found within the working life of a society, an area of activity with other means of communication — the telex and data networks — to fall back on.

It is also fitting in another sense. The first use to which Viewdata has been put in the provision of message services has much to do with English and American welfare preoccupations, and is suitably loaded with cross-Atlantic irony. It is concerned with the provision of a communications medium for the deaf. And if you think we have been here before, you are right: we have, and that was more than a century ago.

Alexander Graham Bell did not set out to invent a telephone: he set out to study the nature of speech and hearing, primarily to enable him to devise better ways to help the deaf.

But the result was the telephone which, far from helping the deaf, made their plight worse. For the dependence of society on the written word and the postal system soon began to decrease. The telephone habit which brings immediacy took hold, and the art of letter writing began to be undermined until we reached the situation we have today where in some societies, notably the Scandinavian, it is much easier to telephone almost anybody — even government ministers — and obtain a response, than write a letter — which the experienced know will seldom be answered in kind.

Now what are the characteristics of communication between the deaf, or between the deaf and non-deaf? Sight is essential between all parties, as is an understanding of the language of the deaf where the conversation is face to face. What is sometimes forgotten, however, is that the deaf learn two sign languages and one of them is the written language used by the rest of us: sight does not necessarily demand 'face to face'. For the deaf also write letters and use the written word, often more than the non-deaf.

It is obvious that Viewdata has relevance here, and that relevance led to the development of the first of the Prestel-Viewdata technology message services. Just three days short of the centenary of Alexander Graham Bell's demonstration of the telephone to Queen Victoria at Osborne House on the Isle of Wight, the Post Office gave a demonstration of Prestel for the deaf.

The demonstration, on 11 January 1978, again took place at Osborne House. Ambitiously, it was not a local demonstration, but a translantic one. The *dramatis personae* had been carefully chosen: on one side in the Isle of Wight, its Lieutenant Governor, Queen Victoria's grandson, the Earl Mountbatten of Burma — a perhaps more appropriate choice than most of the audience knew, as Earl Mountbatten's initial service reputation in the Royal Navy of the 1920s and the 1930s was as a communications specialist; on the other side in the British Embassy in Washington, Bell's great granddaughter Mrs Lillian Grosvenor Jones, and Dr Latham Breunig,

President of the Alexander Graham Bell Association for the Deaf.

The demonstration suffered the trauma associated with such occasions: misstarts, breaks in service — most of which had little to do with Viewdata itself — and was full of keyboard errors. What was shown however gave a flavour of a message service with interesting characteristics. As devised, the message application showed a split screen, the top half displaying the outgoing message, the bottom half the returning message. As both messages grew, so the top line in each was removed, so that the last thought and part of the communication was always displayed.

The system carried a prompt, a kind of visual version of the bleep or the 'over' signal found in radio communications — armed services press-to-talk phones, Citizens' Band and the like — so that each user could see whose turn it was to transmit. This is in fact a key facility, for there can be a tendency to assume, particularly in societies in which people have been brought up on the written word, that the Viewdata communication is one that is written, and the user might well go into writing mode, with its particular forms, salutations and the like, all of which have a greater degree of redundancy than the spoken work can be made to have.

While clearly this mode of conversation is not as fast as spoken dialogue (the necessity to be able to type and type quickly will see to that), nevertheless it can be quite effective. It is of course effective in the absence of anything better, and currently there *is* nothing better.

It is obvious that such a system is capable of considerable development. The demonstration demanded that there was a Viewdata computer in the middle, but clearly it is not essential to such a communication that there should be any computer in the transmission path at all. It is possible to arrange terminals so that they can communicate directly, and the more intelligent the terminal, the more easily can the communication be made.

However, there are two great advantages to having the Viewdata computer in the circuit. The first is to be found in a recurring theme of this book, one for which no apology is required: economy. One can use a standard Viewdata terminal which has a alpha-numeric keyboard, and hence economies of scale apply here as elsewhere.

Secondly, the computer in the circuit introduces order into what could otherwise be a difficult situation to control. There is little difficulty with one conversation: with thousands it could be otherwise. The computer is not simply used as a switch, it is a store and forward device, a transducer, one which limits the amount of special purpose know-how and instructions that would otherwise have to be built into the terminals.

The conversation in the Isle of Wight-Washington link was an ordered dialogue, with one 'speaker' transmitting at any one time. This is not necessarily the conversation of the future since the medium was and is two-way. It would have been and will be possible, for the system to be so arranged that interruptions take place; the separation of the two parts of the conversation on the screen indeed makes this quite easy for the user to grapple with, and turns that ordered, structured and somewhat artificial two-way message system into something more analogous to a normal conversation, which will in turn tend to drive the structure of the dialogue in the direction of the spoken rather than the written word, even though it is the written word that is being dealt with.

Conclusion

This chapter has considered the structure of communications possible with Viewdata. It should have become apparent in this discussion that a Viewdata national system has generality in that it can deal with any type of communication that the user cares to initiate (except of course the bulk transmission of goods not reducible to paper!) and in any form.

If we take the generality within the sphere of information retrieval and within communications, can these two be allied to specifics to produce new kinds of services?

The question alone predicates the answer: of course. How generality can be turned into specifics and what specifics look immediately likely is the concern of the next part of this book. We begin with the movement of money, the role of Viewdata in electronic funds transfer.

4 Electronic funds transfer

To understand the role of Viewdata systems within electronic funds transfer, one must first of all understand electronic funds transfer — EFT — as it exists, and how and why it has developed. The notion of EFTS (S standing for system/s) is now old, having been with us since the early sixties. It stems from the concept of 'The Cashless Society' — CS — an idea which first began to be seriously discussed in the USA during the heyday of the Kennedy Administration, and crossed the Atlantic shortly thereafter. Those were the days when, naïvely perhaps, all things were still thought of as possible, even if not all were likely.

The cashless society as a concept and EFTS as the mechanism by which it could come about were the result of the introduction of digital computing in the banking and money-control institutions, and of the involvement of the money men with fast electronic communications.

The CS and EFTS were both seized on, often by those who should know better, as directions in which to move. That private personal cash which does not have to be accounted for to others helps to give freedom was neither discussed nor noticed. Money after all does not require identity documents nor does the payee need to provide personal data when settling a transaction (or rather, *should* not), while the use of cheques or credit cards leaves behind an originator trace which can be used, probably against the payee.

It was not, however, philosophers, social engineers/politicians who made the running; rather it was seen as a probable source of revenue and profit by systems manufacturers and money-handling institutions, who immediately started to see if they could identify the initially profitable-looking parts.

But how did the notion arise in the first place? With the exceptions noted earlier, one cannot point to a single original thinker making a conceptual leap and saying: this is the way we should go. Rather, the notion of EFT grew from an extension of existing habit. It is sometimes, indeed often, forgotten that money is as precise a form of information as you can have. Money and the recording of what had or was happening to it had been the initial commercial base of computing, for money was particularly susceptible to digital treatment.

Digital techniques

Digital techniques had and still have many implications on the handling and recording of money. Three were of particular importance here. First — and of course — they encouraged a particular habit of mind in their users. Briefly, their use makes it possible for the users of computer systems in finance to think in terms of costs of transactions; computing makes it possible to break costs down and properly attribute them. The more digital techniques move in, the easier this becomes, though previously the costs might have been very difficult to identify because they were spread over so many widely distributed manual and machine functions.

Now the computing-related ability to identify the specific transaction-related costs involved gave the banks an element of control. But only a small element. Of equal importance, it illustrated that the banks had little control over money-handling costs in the rest of the money chain system. The solutions seemed obvious: if digital technology could bring clarity to the centre, the way the banks saw themselves, surely it could eventually do it right across the board?

The second element had to do not only with control, but also with growth. It was seen that the use of computer systems made growth possible. There is an old story that had automatic switching not been invented, the Bell telephone system would by now employ every female in the United States to connect up subscribers one with another. The banks seemed to face a similar problem.

The classic example, of course, is the UK clearing bank system, with the main banks having branches on thousands of street corners. It was seen that an increase in transaction volumes without extensive reliance on systems would lead to a great increase in manpower, yet there was nowhere that manpower could be placed. Growth with new volumes was not possible without a change in administrative working and the use of computing technology. Initially, that would not so much reduce employed manpower as increase the volumes it could handle.

The third element was technological: the banks saw that the existing technology was limited, but also thought that the technology requirement could be invented. The systems that the money institutions would require to bring a set of EFTS into being were dependent upon telecommunications, new hardware, new software, an immense amount of effort into systems design, security, privacy, and changes both in habit and law within society. EFT systems, in other words, were a long-term set of solutions to handling the ever-increasing volumes of information. The use of the phrase 'set of solutions' is important, for it soon became apparent that it was not a question of one EFT system but a number, each built to handle a specific function or set of functions. It was not a question of saying that we will have EFTS and thus the Cashless Society — the latter dropped out in serious discussion quite quickly as it became apparent that some of the problems involved were intractable; there were no systems solutions in sight even if society was prepared to let the banks and money men go that way — by such and such a date; rather it became a question of which system could be put up most easily, each coming up on an individual basis.

The development of EFT systems has not been anywhere near as tidy as this might lead one to suppose, for the technology has not behaved as expected. However, even if the cashless society is still a pipe dream, some forms of EFT are already in use and others at various stages of development

EFT and the cashless society

The initial forms were those which gave the highest pay-off for the minimum disturbance, large payment transactions between banks themselves, and the handling of payments which had regularity. However, at the heart of the notion of 'The Cashless Society' lay the idea that EFT systems could be devised which would replace conventional payments systems such as cash, cheques; that the individual would accept the direct debit/credit of the account by electronics at the time the transaction was made and payment authorised. The system would capture the data, and then make the appropriate information transfer.

We have been quite scathing about the notion of 'The Cashless Society', not only because it implies social engineering on a massive scale, without thought as to whether the society wishes that engineering to take place, but also because much of the talk of a cashless society discloses only first-order thinking on the consequences of the proposed actions: it was not seriously rooted in reality.

The reality is that people like cash, and that the more the State involves itself in the affairs of individuals, the more they prefer to keep as many as possible of their financial transactions out of sight of the authorities. This distrust is understandable and healthy. A standard estimate made by those within the banking system is that there is in the UK between £1500 and £2000 million 'out there', cash which never seems to return to the banks. How much of that float is the cash which keeps the black economy, that part which operates without benefit or otherwise of the taxman, nobody knows.

Electronic funds transfer

At the officially known level, cash in the UK still accounts for 90 to 95 per cent of all financial transactions. Half the UK's employees are still paid weekly in cash, and half the adults do not as yet have a bank account. When you add it all up, you find that less than 10 per cent of society's money exchange transactions go through the banks and other formal money exchange 'market' institutions.

Perhaps as important, the few studies made of the ways in which people with bank accounts actually use them indicate that they behave differently from those who simply use cash. The majority actively manage their money and their payments. For instance, whereas the majority of those paying their utility bills in cash do so within ten days, the majority of those paying by cheque take up to six weeks to pay. The notion that the people are easily manipulable in the interests of the efficiency, economy and profit of those who set up or wish to set up EFT systems, has turned out to be wrong. Given the choice, people behave like the institutions: they wish for the maximum velocity of money in and the minimum velocity of money out.

We write about the UK: enquiries — not in any great depth — in the USA, France and Germany indicate that where people generally have the chance to behave as if the system was set up in their interest, they tend to do so. And one should not expect anything different.

However, in the UK, EFT systems continue to grow. Indeed, because of the national bank structure of the UK's money-handling mechanisms the various experts estimate that the UK is some five to ten years ahead of US practice, if 'ahead' is the way you want to look at it. It has grown in those transaction areas which the money institutions are the best equipped to handle: transactions between themselves, and between them and their large customers, in the clearing of cheques and payments where the banks play a transfer role and in areas easy to identify, automate, and with a high pay off.

It is obvious then that there are massive sections of the money transaction field untouched, most of them also as yet unexplored. Thus, in the UK again it is known that not far short of 50 per cent of all financial transactions using the banking mechanism are from individuals to other individuals, organisations or government, and mostly to the two latter. In the real world of all transactions of course the volumes and percentages are much higher.

Surely then there must be a way of cutting down on a chain which runs: originate cheque, send it, receive it, pay it in, send cheque to originator's bank, make appropriate entries throughout and cancel them if for any reason payment is not finally made, the records finally appearing on a bank Any improvements here could be of direct and immediate benefit to both sides.

What has largely been absent from the EFTS discussion or its realisation has been any sort of system which would give the individual a way of breaking that chain electronically, one which would give people the ability the banks have also to authorise electronically payments to others, whether individuals or organisations, and to obtain on demand the all-important data that a financial transaction has, or has not, happened. There is of course one form of this in use: point-of-sale terminals in retail stores will directly debit from a customer's bank account. The terminal is not the customer's, and the advantage does not seem to be in favour of the payee except where the store gives a discoung for getting the cash directly into its account.

However, when you turn to the notion of the terminal in the home, this side of the literature is almost non-existent. For up till now no-one has been able to foresee a home terminal that users would be willing to pay for which would give them any sort of EFTS capability.*

It is this situation, this possible market, on which Viewdata technology could well impact. As discussed at length elsewhere Viewdata could make the jump into the home economically possible. This jump, however, is not a simple one; but is so complex that the banks — in the UK at least — have as yet hardly looked at it.

---

* As we correct the manuscript, reports have come in of one experiment being monitored in the USA (June 1979).

Let us begin with some conventional possibilities: the substitution of EFT/Viewdata type services for existing bank services, the territory opened up by the substitution of home on-line electronic systems for a paper, post and personal call system.

Now it has already been observed that the public seems to like dealing with electronic devices for financial transactions: such devices give an illusion of privacy. The automated bank teller seems to have the same characteristics as the automated medical history enquiry system. People are more likely both to tell the truth, in the sense that they state what really worries them, and to take the advice or information given at its face value: they are not distracted by person-to-person signals, nor do they have to pay attention to the other party's psychological make-up and whether or not they like them, for the only other party present is a machine. This is obviously a plus sign for those who might seek to market such a system.

EFT/Viewdata as substitute

So what bank services could EFT/Viewdata substitute for?

There is no intrinsic reason why a Viewdata user should not have available a facility to interrogate his bank's Viewdata computing system about his account. Details of the account would not be kept on the Viewdata service, but would be called down when required. Some software to make this possible, to translate the enquiry from one form into another, already exists at the general level. This is account-holder initiated enquiry.

Nor is there any intrinsic reason why it should not work the other way around: why the bank's system should not be able to initiate a conversation with an account holder notifying him/her that such and such a payment has now been made, that his/her account has been credited with the following, that a payment is now due, that interest has been credited or debited to/from the following, or indeed notify the customer at agreed intervals of the state of the account to a previously defined level of detail.

It will be noticeable that the procedures so far outlined are no more than a substitution of Viewdata for existing and current bank procedures, whether one is substituting Viewdata for the use of the mail system, or one type of computing system (though with a much larger population of on-line terminals) for another. Though of course as the new terminal population will be outside the bank or the regular banking system, new — and perhaps different — security procedures will have to be devised. However, there is nothing in the above list which the banking community would find in essence unfamiliar.

But how difficult would any of these services be to provide? In principle, they are quite easy; indeed, most could be handled on Viewdata Mark One, *sans* printer, storage, intelligence or alpha numeric keypad. (Though obviously a statement of accound service in full detail would be immeasurably helped by a printer, this particular facility is unlikely to come about in the public market until the terminal population has the facility to enable the data to be taken off and run at leisure, which means local storage and printers.)

But which service might we actually see? It is obvious that the banks will initially go for bank-initiated dialogues: their worries about security are such that, particularly in the UK, they would need considerable convincing, as well as systems experience, before considering a customer-originated dialogue which does much more than ask general questions. Certainly, until they had a better understanding of the security requirement in practice, they would not provide a service which gave access to details of a 'live' account or allowed payments to be initiated by a customer at will.

How might a bank go about it? Skip all the data about provision of the system's facilities at the bank's end and assume that there is a bank-customer Prestel Viewdata terminal population out in the field.

Initially the bank writes to its customers asking if they have a Viewdata terminal, and offering some of the facilities described as part of its service, via Viewdata. It offers data on account items which have regularity, specific movements in and out of an account on fixed dates: interest paid on deposit accounts, and interest debited on loans and overdrafts to be notified once a quarter, or as credited/debited. The bank also offers to give the account balance at the end of each such record of a debit/credit transaction.

What is offered is a bank-initiated, restricted, preset dialogue. There is no further enquiry facility: the user cannot ask for further details to be made accessible via Viewdata, though a specific input can be used to ensure additional details by post.

Stage two extends the facility: with experience the banks are prepared to allow the customer to initiate a conversation with the bank's Viewdata systems. Initially this is during working hours, but then it is seen that they are not so limited, that in fact Viewdata — being computer dependent — can be used more positively as part of the bank's marketing at any hour. The facility now allows for detailed statements to be sought for, initially following the same path as the banks themselves do for an internal enquiry, last six movements in and out of the account and balance.

We are now of course some years into the eighties, and Viewdata terminals with printers are becoming standard, so that the next stage is obvious: the full detailed statement can be made available either on demand or at prearranged regular intervals.

We have not so far really been discussing EFTS at all, but still considering the transfer of existing bank information services from one medium — paper — and method of transmission — the post — to another, Viewdata. This is a necessary prelude to some form of EFTS: indeed one can argue that the banks themselves did not consider EFTS until they had got into a position where financial account data was kept up on computer systems in digital form. For if you are to operate at electronic speeds, then all the *necessary* data must be kept in the same form: keeping books on two media which have different operating time scales seldom works satisfactorily.

Where then might EFTS begin?

Viewdata and EFTS

Among the early experimental databases put up was one by British Airways which gave the airline's timetable and holiday offerings. This included a booking facility enabling the user to decide what offering he wanted to take up, confirm and book, for the booking page was followed by a confirmation page carrying at the bottom right-hand a prompt for the entry of a credit card number.

The implications of that are many, for if an airline can sell directly via Viewdata with a hook-up to the source of funds, whether or not these come directly from the user, so can travel agents, direct-mail houses, indeed almost any marketing organisation which has enough to offer to make it economic to try to move it via Viewdata.

However, such sales in their full generality are not possible on the Prestel-Viewdata service as currently running; they depend on the full development of response frames.

Response frames, though not yet fully and finally developed, have one characteristic: they ask the user to input information into Viewdata which will then be passed on elsewhere. This in turn requires an organised, routine, on-line connection between the Prestel-Viewdata computers within the network and the Information Provider concerned.

This is obviously important in the airline booking case: the flight requested, for instance, may be full in the particular class sought by the user. True, there is no technological reason why the airline should not provide Prestel-Viewdata's computers with a continuous automatic update of flight and holiday availability, and this no doubt will eventually happen. But it is some years off since it depends upon some very specific systems arrangements being made: the writing of software, link creation, etc. All these will of course involve extra costs. One does not expect to see cross linking of this degree until the terminal population in the field is quite large.

As discussed then, the system would depend on the airlines running such a service inputting updated flight availability and other information at frequent daily intervals. It would require some sort of simple connection between Prestel Viewdata computers and the airline system, so that the airline can come back with confirmation or otherwise.

This would get the user through the response frames. For the next stage, an on-line link is required between the airline and the credit card company's system to confirm — or not — the specific transaction. Put like this, neither are difficult to arrange.

We have not of course eliminated the postal system: though the booking may have become 'electronic' and the process of payment may have had the paper-slip-signing ceremony removed from it, the ticket still has to be originated by the airline and sent to the passenger. However, the paper process has been at least reduced.

Is there a possibility of eliminating it entirely? Currently, and as long as airlines issue tickets which are printed on paper, the answer seems to be no. The reason has to do with the problems of security. Exclude the notion of doing away with tickets entirely: there are hosts of reasons why this is not practicable. The economics of current printer technology are such that it would be difficult to conceive of a printing mechanism which could produce something not easily duplicable. We are then faced with the possibility of fraud.

Of course, there are other ways of coping with this elimination of paper problem; however these are outside the context of a discussion of Viewdata and forms of EFTS: they depend on administrative changes in organisations, changes which may one day come about but are of little relevance to a discussion of Viewdata's progress over the next few years.

Viewdata: other uses

The combination of response frames could lead to other uses in the financial field, and a couple of examples are worth considering.

Take the credit card example, and at the entry point substitute for credit card number your bank account number. There is no reason why banks should not eventually provide a direct debit facility of their own between the account holder and a supplier of goods and services.

Then there is the sale of banks' own goods and services: money and financial information. The use of response frames could lead to the banks offering loans specifically tailored to their customers' needs — the preliminary enquiry, total amount to be borrowed, time over which to be repaid, instalments, interest charged all being dealt with via Viewdata-type systems.

All that we have written in this chapter is possible: which parts will come about and in what time scale it is difficult to evaluate. For if anything in this book is set in the future, it has been these words on Viewdata and EFTS. Though one of the uses we have described, the airline/credit card use, has been demonstrated, it remains a fact that at the time of writing not one real and live EFTS transaction has so far been carried by Viewdata. There is only an intent by major organisations some time in the future to utilise Viewdata in this way.

5 Education

Though never quantified — or if so, undiscovered despite search — there appears to be a correlation between economic growth, the cut in the working week, and the increase in the number and breadth of services which can be called 'educational'. Leisure with income after all, as is well known, breeds a desire and demand for educational services, whether the education is examination-bound in the hope of economic reward, or arises from a need to add almost immediate skills or solve a problem: 'I have always wanted to know about this or that but, for whatever reason, I never had the time before.' 'How do I fix this carburettor, learn enough of that language in order to be polite to the natives?' 'Why are my lettuces always so scrawny when my neighbour's are not?'

What then has Viewdata technology to offer those at both ends of the educational chain, the purveyors and the would-be learners? Well, almost all that we have written so far about the technology's characteristics and capabilities applies. It is user-oriented and user-initiated (though the call-in-sequence facility discussed in the chapter on communications services could have applications in education as it could do for many other services). It has immediacy, which in educational services can be all-important in that replies come best while the would-be learner is actually thinking around the subject he/she is enquiring about. It could in some circumstances therefore have an immense advantage over paper and post communications systems, though obviously at the present stage of development the facilities would be fairly limited. And of course, once a national network exists, there is a possibility of immense potential available — the ability to test new applications quickly, indeed instantaneously if desired. The notion of testing information services as they are being developed is not a new one, but it becomes more easily and economically possible with electronic media, and Viewdata bids fair to be the largest two-way electronic medium of them all.

Viewdata and education

Education of course is in large part about information transfer, and since this forms the basis of information retrieval, educational services would seem a natural development. But is there anything else that the system can do which was not done before and which would help when it comes to seeking educational aid?

Firstly there is the ability of Viewdata systems to be so constructed as to present only the information sought at any particular time; the ability to select a window size and view. The user therefore thinks of himself as being 'in charge', even though the conduct of a dialogue with the system will run along a set of predictable possibilities. The interaction between user and system is such that the term user is itself redundant; he/she becomes a participant.

Next, one should not underestimate the ability of a national network as a disseminator of national data, particularly where the information was previously only regional in character, though not necessarily by design or intent, simply because of the lack of media. That same national characteristic becomes particularly useful in subjects where though the majority of the data is the same this week as last, yet critical components have changed.

There are two other characteristics of Viewdata systems which can apply and which are of immense value in education, whether or not the system put up is a national one.

There is the characteristic that a terminal viewed and operated in the home can be conversed with on a one-to-one basis: if you make a fool of yourself, nobody else need know. This previously mentioned characteristic should not be underestimated. As indicated in the discussion on EFT systems, man-machine dialogue studies in other related fields have shown that people are freer, behave more naturally and become more immersed in what they are doing (including being truthful) when left to work with systems on their own.

There is also the characteristic which Viewdata shares with other computer systems designed for a genuine two-way interaction. The participant can assess the results of trying out a particular approach or strategy very quickly, *as can the system*. This may not seem obvious, but has considerable implications; indeed it becomes apparent that in much of conventional learning where a teacher teaches and the pupils listen, Viewdata — like all properly devised digital systems — is a far superior method of imparting information.

It is characteristic of on-line computer systems that all but the final piece of relevant information for assessment can be captured prior to the user's answer, and that this information can then be so arranged and made available that seemingly instantaneous analysis results. 'In the sum $224 \times 321 \div 33$, you went wrong at the following step...'

The system can also be arranged so as to operate in reverse, so that the participant can be asked to express opinions and views. Initially one would expect this to happen on the system's initiation, with the system putting up prearranged comment, a menu of items from which to pick. Was the test difficult, very difficult, almost impossible, or too easy? Which of the listed parts of the test caused you problems, and would you like to try those parts again, or call for more information? Press the appropriate number at the side of the item concerned, for further instruction. The point is that the system can capture the feelings of the participant while they are still fresh in his or her mind.

So what, more specifically, can Viewdata do within education? What sort of applications can we expect to see?

Educational applications

First come the applications in which Viewdata takes over for one reason or another from existing computer-based systems, applications where a transfer is likely whether on grounds of economy or an increase in user population because the terminals can become cheaply and widely available. One should not forget here how education can actually operate: often kit is not bought because it is too expensive, or because its expensiveness is such that a procedure has to be gone through prior to purchase. Much computing equipment is currently being bought in the UK, particularly within the educational sector, simply because the fall in prices set against performance has been such that it comes within the budget of the educational establishment without requiring that anyone else be consulted. Above a thousand pounds, say, a committee has to be approached; below this figure the purchase comes within the purchasing responsibilities of the headmaster (or whoever) without necessitating any further clearance.

An instance of a transfer which is related to the first sentence of the above paragraph is Britain's Open University. This is currently a substantial supplier of conventional computer terminals, used by students. In comparison with Viewdata terminals, these have been quite expensive to buy, and have not had a good colour graphics capability. However, the Open University has become committed to Viewdata technology for its future system, for it can now face an interesting prospect. As the general Viewdata terminal population begins to grow across the whole population, so the OU may be able to cut terminals entirely out of its budget, allowing for an expansion of *services* to a greatly increased population who will purchase their own terminals.

Within this same area of transfer of existing systems is to be found what is a standard use in the USA, though not as yet all that common in Europe — the computer system used for educational administration, allocating classes, dates, times and the like. Here Viewdata technology makes a rapid growth in such usage a possibility, but it also does so on a general population basis. It can allow for the wide dissemination of data on what classes in what subjects are available at which educational institutions (school, college), what qualifications are required, together with course description, recommended reading and the minutiae of course application — dates by which various steps have to be taken, what combinations of subjects or courses are possible, and so on and so on.

This sort of search lends itself particularly well to the systems described and the dialogues the technology can handle, the step-by-step approach. Expressed in one sentence, the system could easily answer a question of the following type: 'I have the following school-leaving examination passes (known in the UK as 'O' and 'A' Levels) of the following grades. Do I qualify to study medicine, and if so, to what University could I go? Which of these has a place available for the term beginning...?'

An area of great importance in which Viewdata could impact on the educational system is in the dissemination of course material itself, whether localised, within a school, a college, or generally available on the national system direct to the home. The availability of course material in this way could have a substantial impact: that such material could be easily obtainable on demand may strike those committed to the concept of a formal educational system as strange, yet a strong case can be made for it.

In Europe particularly, children — sometimes quite young — face homework. It is for instance quite possible that a million or more parents in the UK will be asked every week night during term-time for help with homework, help which they cannot for some reason or another give: they don't know, they have forgotten, there are no aids in the home, or they are busy. In many cases they are ashamed that they do not know. One of us has been saying for three years that Viewdata technology could be of enormous benefit if, say, an encyclopaedia publisher put up a special version geared to the schools' examination syllabuses. For example, this could not only give the papers set by the examining boards in mathematics, physics, biology* for the last five years, but also help in working them out (see immediately below).

CAL

Traditionally, or at least for the last twenty years or so, there has been considerable talk (and some serious work) on computer-aided instruction, commonly known by its initials CAI. Viewdata technology, though limited in that, for instance, the on-line power available is not large — and is likely to be thus limited on a public network for a long time to come — opens up another territory, one which those involved in the field of computers in education consider the next step. Its name is computer-aided *learning* (CAL) which puts the main emphasis on the individual than the system, whether the educational system or the technological system.

The ability to make use of the individual's characteristics and not to be confined to timetables and/or working hours — in other words, the time independence brought about by the inexpensiveness of the technology — should not be underestimated, particularly when allied to techniques enabling the learning processes to work with electronic systems, techniques on which much work has been done on both sides of the Atlantic.

Thus the use of subject matter structures and their links, both in terms of subject matter and how it can be used; sophisticated versions of multiple-choice question techniques; modelling of real-life situations (all with the feedback that digital communications technology makes possible) — many of these have already been experimented with on Viewdata. The

---

* One should not ignore the humanities. However, English literature papers, for instance, would probably require greater screen capacity and we do not envisage this side taking off until 2000-character screens are the norm.

technology has even been used to simulate laboratory conditions, in which experiments can be carried out, the results observed and commented upon by the system. One splendid experimental laboratory — choice 9 below — demonstrates clinical knowledge, and it is not unusual for the student to be informed that he or she has managed to kill the patient! Thus the student can go on experimenting electronically until he or she 'gets it right', before proceeding to treat real patients.

CAL involves, of course, the interactive capabilities of Viewdata, which enable the student to make responses, those responses to be assessed, and the results of the assessments to be instantaneously provided to reinforce understanding or assist in self-correction.

The entry point to the section on experimental education programmes gives a glimpse of the possibilities of Viewdata in this CAI/CAL:

 0 An Experiment in Programmed Learning
 1 Junior School Topics
 2 Multiple choice questions
 3 CAI Under Task Control
 4 Examination/Revision Notes
 5 Graded Quizzes
 6 Previous Examination Papers
 7 Computer Aided Instruction
 8 The Laboratory on the Screen
 9 Decision Making in Medicine

Choice 0 is a conventional programmed-learning text on calorimetry, making substantial use of graphics. As is now standard practice in programmed-learning material, tuition is interspersed with test questions which enable the student to check whether he has fully understood the text with all its implications. The checking program is simple: a repetition of the same wrong answers sends the student back to study the text once again. However, at present no attempt is made to diagnose what the student's difficulties with the text may be, and much could be done in this respect. To round off the learning programme at choice 0, a set of multiple-choice questions is available (under option 2), covering the same ground but with a new set of test questions. Finally, the score is added up to give a measure of the student's performance in his or her understanding of the entire text.

A departure from the standard programmed learning text is choice 3, Computer Aided Instruction Under Task Control, which is an instruction text on elementary thermodynamics dealing with the steam engine and turbine. It is based on the now well accepted theory of the 'entailment structure' concept developed by Professor Gordon Pask.* Here a subject is broken down into a number of sub-topics, showing their interrelations; understanding of the sub-topics and their relationships to the main topic is an essential element in the true understanding of the whole subject.

The course begins with a presentation of the topics and their interrelations, shown graphically in a topic map; then the student is invited to select a topic with which to begin the 'study'. As with programmed learning, a short quiz is presented at the end of every basic step, which if successfully answered returns the student to the topic map offering the remaining topics for further selection. Thus the student has full control of the path taken to explore the subject, picking on whichever item appears most attractive or appealing at any time; the computer is programmed to indicate on the topic map which choices remain to be completed to obtain an understanding of the whole. The student feels that he/she is collaborating closely with an intelligent supervisor intensely interested in his/her progress. Experiments carried out by Systems Research, the company responsible for the program, have indicated that it was much liked by young children who enjoyed the interactive capability of the system and the high speed of response, though at this stage Viewdata has only been programmed to deal with task structures in a simple way.

Among the most immediately striking demonstrations of the capability of Viewdata in education are choices 8 and 9. Choice 8, the 'laboratory on the screen', simulates a modelling

---

* With whom one of the authors, Rex Malik, is associated.

situation in which a student can conduct an actual — though simple — experiment on a machine as if the experiment was taking place in a real laboratory. The experiment hardly needs the elaboration of a real laboratory or indeed of Viewdata to carry it out; a simple rule, pencil and a few small coins would have been quite adequate, but the potential for more complex experiments and artefacts is there. Indeed it is not too difficult to conceive experiments which it would be physically impossible to carry out in a classroom or even in a well equipped laboratory, such as verifying the exact thrust of a moon rocket for a successful moon shot; yet these could be handled by Viewdata. The experiment at Choice 8 is intended to teach the principle of moments which underlies the working of simple machines — levers, multiple pulleys etc. — by making it possible to adjust the weights placed at the ends of a lever so as to obtain an exact balance, the lever tilting one way if the weight added is too low and the other way if it is too high. The sequence shown illustrates a typical chain of events.

Far more spectacular, because of its emotional human overtones, is Choice 9: Decision Making in Medicine. This is based on experiments and programmes designed at the Glasgow University, and was previously referred to. One of the programmes illustrated is the 'Emergency situation model' which is clearly not an experiment which can be carried out on real people. Indeed, in this simulation the student may step back from a situation in which a recommended treatment has caused the death of an imaginary patient, and can retrace one or more steps before finally applying the successful remedy.

In the emergency simulation programme the student is presented with a crisis in which rapid decisions are needed, and may select from a number of courses of action and treatments. The condition of the patient then improves or deteriorates accordingly, and ultimately he either dies or his condition stabilises.

The patient in this particular case is a self-employed businessman, aged about 47, well-built but appearing shocked, pale, sweating and confused. The initial physical examination indicates a high pulse rate associated with low blood pressure, which indicates a heart/blood volume complication. Further examination also reveals a malfunction of the liver. The heart condition is critical and while treatment is administered to cope with it, further investigation of the liver continues, a close watch being maintained on the heart rate/blood pressure combination.

A misinterpretation of the patient's condition results in the giving of a dose of digoxin, which in the event proves lethal and results in cardiac arrest. The alternative choice, dieuretics treatment, would have saved the patient.

The potential of this approach to the teaching of all subjects, particularly complex subjects such as medicine, is clearly immense. It is not the *only* approach possible; but it *is* the first time such an approach could be realisable on a system readily available to a large audience.

6 Viewdata as calculator

We are in this section concerned with Viewdata in a public network system; with Viewdata technology in use in a public computer utility such as Prestel. We are not concerned with private Viewdata systems, where it is obvious that the computing power available is under the control of the user — whether organisation or individual. The user can put up as much power as he is willing to pay for, and can write or have written software to make the Viewdata system behave as a very powerful computation facility — if the power is there.

That the computers within a public Prestel-type system are capable of being used for calculation and computation is obvious. They are no different from computers employed for standard computing and general-purpose data manipulation, whether these are the GEC 4080s supplied to the British Post Office or others which would fill the same role. It is of course true that computers devised specifically for rapid computation can include features not found in the 4080, special hardware for fast Fourier transforms, and separate attached processors to facilitate computations requiring a large amount of parallel working if they are to be handled effectively. But it is unlikely that those who wish to carry out such calculations would think of doing so via a public computer utility network. Indeed, for some simple floating point operations one would do better with a calculator.

This is a good point to remind the reader that Viewdata

technology has taken some years to be brought to fruition, and that in this time considerable technological change has occurred.

There have been two developments which take the load off the notion that a network service might have to provide extensive computational ability. Both are integrated circuit based. One is the calculator itself, the other is the microprocessor.

Computing costs are falling by about fifty per cent every five years. This applies equally to small stand-alone computers, whether for business or for personal use, and to the computers used for Viewdata. At first sight it might seem that the provision of the substantial power in a Viewdata centre, with a not inconsiderable memory attached and substantial software development behind it — all this at a cost to be shared among many tens, perhaps hundreds of thousands of daily users — should tip the balance in favour of the network solution. However, we doubt that this will actually happen. We believe that the scales will eventually tilt in favour of the small stand-alone computer, for the same reasons that the Viewdata network itself is headed in the direction of a distributed mesh of computers: the cost of communications.

This does not mean that, as Viewdata is currently being established, Viewdata systems are incapable of meeting some computational needs. We consider those needs, dependent on appropriate product development and marketing policies, to be two in number. Computationally simple applications specifically tailored to particular applications which can be run on-line from the Prestel Viewdata computer and plugged in to the network on demand; and the off-loading from that network of called-down computational programs stored in some device on the Viewdata receiver terminal. These are then run in an attached (or built into the Viewdata terminal) microprocessor, one which gives more power than the standard facility of the first terminal model type, and which has been devised to take those programs.

Calculation programs

An example of the first type of calculations possible without an attached microprocessor are the mortgage calculation programs already available (though only on an experimental basis as we write) on Prestel. Two options are provided. Given the capital sum that has been borrowed, the interest charged and a stated level of repayment, it calculates the duration of the loan. Given the sum borrowed, the duration of the loan and the rate of interest, it will calculate the level of repayment.

One useful feature of this program is that it will also provide information on interest levels currently charged by the various mortgage providers, the British building societies, thus facilitating comparisons. Another feature is the checking facility which enables the user to look at the rate at which the loan repayment is being made, and establish the amount of interest and capital so far repaid and what remains outstanding.

These and similar calculation exercises could easily be extended to enable links to be drawn between — for instance — mortgage loans and endowment insurance, and the effects of taxation on the net repayment options available, given different levels of income and tax.

The second area initially takes us to what has been called Telesoftware. This was first proposed by William Overington as an additional feature for broadcast Teletext which could be used perhaps during 'the quiet hours'.* The idea is to use those hours to transfer software from central computers to the user's own computer; in this case, the micro of the intelligent Viewdata terminal.

Of course, one need not only transfer programs. Even earlier, the prolific Donald Davies of the UK's National Physical Laboratory had suggested that the broadcast facility

---

* The immediate objection that this could only work in societies where the television system closes down at night, as in most of Europe, is not that serious a problem. Even in the USA, many of the television stations do in fact close down at night, and some networking satellite channels are unused.

be used to transfer data updates between computer systems during the night hours.

Both systems would be easily practicable in the UK. Given that the user is willing to pay the line costs and other charges, there is no intrinsic reason why there should be a restriction to overnight (though bulky transfers which tie up ports for long periods during peak hours could cause problems with poor network design).

Telesoftware is an idea that has been taken up by that leading British software house, CAP-CPP. They look at Viewdata as a system of program, one which for the first time enables software distribution to be marketed on line directly to a mass market. To do this, they have had to go down the route of program portability, for currently few programs devised for one machine will run on another without modification. In the on-line situation with naïve users, modification is — if not impossible — obviously difficult, time consuming and costly.

Of course, some machine efficiency has to be sacrificed to make a software system run on almost any computer or microprocessor. This has not been done for standard mainframe computers, but has however been done for the major manufacturers' microprocessors.

As a serious tool of calculation outside the field of simple pre-programmed packages — such as the mortgage case previously discussed — it is obvious that for the foreseeable future Viewdata technology will be dependent upon intelligent terminals with attached microprocessors. With these the technology should be able to handle anything that can be done on a smallish stand-alone system, as well as many things that cannot, simply by the system's ability to call down from what we expect eventually to be a wide library of calculation programs.

There is however a class of programs on Viewdata, some of which already require a kind of calculation capability. These are probably the first Viewdata programs with which users will work — if it can be called work — and become familiar: games.

7 Viewdata games

From the start, Viewdata games have been the marketing man's dream. During some of the trials of the System Research educational material, the games were used as bribes, though in fact it transpired that bribes were not needed. Do the test, work your way through, and we will let you play a game or two. (It was usually three.) The games have been immensely popular, and habit forming.

Now clearly, playing games with or against a computer is not new. Charles Babbage, the father of computation by mechanical means (though the resemblance is to the electronic computer, the means chosen were mechanical) had the notion that it might be used to play chess and in fact wrote this in 1840. Over 100 years later the idea was taken up by Alan Turing, a mathematician now regarded by many as the father of electronic machine computable mathematics. He was a key (some consider, *the* key) figure in the development of some of the world's first electronic computers, the code-breaking systems of the Foreign Office's Department of Communications at Bletchley, and is reputed to have considered the use of computers to play games. He too picked chess, but there was a war on at the time.

The war over, Turing stated (1949) that he thought it would be a hundred years before a computer could play an average game. Nevertheless, this did not deter him. Three years later he was playing a paper game from rules he had devised; he was playing against a human, but himself behaving exactly according to the rules that would have to be programmed into the computer. For the record, he (the computer) lost at the twenty-ninth move. But this was only fitting, for even as a human, Turing was not a very good chess player.*

Now in case anyone should become enthusiastic at the thought of obtaining a good game out of Viewdata's computers on demand, a little cold water here is necessary.

The snag is that the computer power required to play a game of even moderately high standard chess, say at County level, is as yet exorbitant. It would only take two or three people trying to play chess of this standard against the systems now going into the UK Prestel network, to consume all the power within a centre. Even then it is doubtful if the game would be of the required standard. Moreover it would run counter to the philosophy on which the Viewdata system has been developed: that the use of computer power is minimised in order to achieve as much spread as possible, and devised so as to involve as much of the user's brain power as possible, a sort of man-machine and machine-man dependence, if not initially symbiosis.

However, quite a lot can be done in the games area without the use of much power. Among the initial games giving a semblance of computing-power in use (though this is not so in practice) and which Prestel users have found attractive has been MOO, a variant of Master Mind. In MOO the player has to guess a 4-digit number, the system responding to the guess by giving the numbers of 'bulls' or digits correctly guessed and placed in the right position. The system also responds by giving the number of 'cows', which denote digits correctly guessed but placed in the wrong position.

A different type of game found to have great appeal is the maze game. In this, the player is presented with a maze with one entrance and one exit, and a 'pointer' (a moving electronic marker on the screen) which he can manipulate and move from the entrance to the exit; the number of false moves and the total time taken is recorded and displayed when the

---

* For a fuller description see 'The Machine Plays Chess?' by Alex G Bell, Pergamon Press, 1978.

round is completed. In this game the player is not pitted against computer power. However, handicaps are possible since mazes can be produced with various degrees of complexity according to maze number, the computer producing different mazes even for the same maze number (though each of the same degree of complexity), thus ensuring that mazes and their strategies cannot be memorised.

But are games a viable development for Viewdata? First there is the competition from video games, where for a relatively modest capital outlay many hours of enjoyment can be had without any running costs apart from a charge for electricity. In addition these have a feature that Viewdata, as it now exists, is unlikely to be able to provide; a dynamic and fast response in games like tennis or car racing. While the older type of video game has been found to create only a short-lived interest, newer games based on television-set located microprocessors are a much more formidable competitor. Viewdata, probably unable to compete on costs, might possibly retain the customer who wishes to try a new game on Viewdata before buying the programme cassette or if Viewdata were to develop such an immense library of games programmes that on the score of variety alone it could maintain a competitive stance against cassetted programmes which would be prohibitively expensive if they tried to provide a comparable coverage. Alternatively Viewdata might well become the source of such games programs which could be off-loaded from the system to the user's microprocessor-controlled terminal, after which games playing would be done off-line, with the telephone line to Viewdata disconnected.

But it is in dual games and in group games that Viewdata comes into its own, games in which the participants are not in the same location. Chess has been known to be an ideal game for this treatment, using the telephone line to communicate moves across the players, moves which because of the advanced formalisation of the rules can be easily communicated. Other games have not fared quite so well, probably because of difficulties of description, but even with chess the difficulties are immense and the theoretical possibilities have very seldom been fully realised. For games like chess (and card games like bridge) Viewdata offers new possibilities.

The visual presentation lends itself particularly well to the display of the chessboard, with different colours for the two sides, and to the movement of the pieces which can be made to flash (or even to change colour) to attract the attention of the players. Unlike the situation where the game is played at a distance using the telephone, the state of play is visible to both players at all times and misunderstandings should not arise. The computer could also be programmed to keep a record of the pieces taken by each player, to operate as a time clock, to prompt the players when necessary, and generally ensure that the rules are kept.

Viewdata can also add a further dimension to the playing of chess by supporting multiple games where one player plays several others simultaneously, without confusion (at least on the part of the system) and which, when the central player decides to make a move on a particular board, can retrieve and display that board and immediately transmit the move to the opponent, wherever he might be.

There is however one particular feature of chess by Viewdata which provides the potential for development in a completely new direction, that of enabling other people to watch the progress of the game, unhindered by distance, thus bringing international chess championships to a vast audience across the globe.

What however of the cost? Is this not likely to be prohibitive? Clearly, if one wanted to keep a line open between New York and Moscow for hours on end, it would cost a great deal. However, in chess as a spectator sport the cost could be shared amongst the many watchers, thus reducing the cost per viewer to an acceptable level. Further economies are possible such as, for instance, only activating the telephone connection whenever a move has taken place, instead of leaving the line open continuously even when not conveying any traffic.

It has already become apparent that, with a game like chess which involves fairly long inactive periods and short, active intervals, the present mode of communications between terminal and computer is far from ideal. Packet switching which is being implemented vigorously in many countries, is intended to cope with just such a situation by arranging that traffic between any two points is carried out in a series of bursts of data or 'packets', interleaved with other packets of data from other users sharing parts of the same communications channels. This makes it possible to share a given communication path amongst several users, rather than just two, consequently achieving a substantially higher utilisation of plant and reduced cost to each user. Telenet, one of the packet-switching systems currently in operation in the US, charges about $3 per hour for connections between any two points in the US at any time of day or night; by contrast, a circuit-switched continuous connection lasting one hour would cost $20 in the UK over distances in excess of 56 km.

In a packet-switching system the connection between the individual user and the local telephone exchange, or junction point to the packet-switching system, is still (and probably will remain for some time) dedicated entirely to one user only, the sharing between users taking place between exchanges or junction points, since clearly it is only between these points that there are sufficient users to share a channel. Concentrators which bundle many users' lines may also be introduced between groups of users and the nearest exchange, since in this case it is possible to take advantage of the fact that some users require the communication facility when others do not.

With further development in the application of microprocessors in the Viewdata receiver, even the local call connection charge could be reduced substantially, for example by releasing the line when it is not required to carry traffic and thus emulating the packet-switching concept in the local network.

Teletext

The application of Viewdata to games such as chess, or other kinds of card and board games which might interest a large audience, suggests that in these circumstances there could be a useful marriage between Viewdata and (the broadcast information service) Teletext.

Thus while Teletext has a much smaller information capacity than Viewdata (a few hundred pages compared with possibilities running into millions) it can impart this information to a very high proportion of the total viewing population at the same time. This factor could provide the reason for a connection between the two technologies, which in the game of chess for example could provide a useful additional broadcast low-cost facility for the spectator, while the transmission of the information and the game supervision could be done with Viewdata. In addition a considerable amount of background information, which fewer viewers would require, could also be available on Viewdata, switching from one medium to the other being a simple matter. Other information, such as the sequence of moves, commentaries by chess critics, items of interest to the more dedicated chess watchers, could also be called up in the same way. With the increasing elaboration and sophistication of the Viewdata receiver, additional features will be available to the player and watcher of chess, such as the ability to recall one or more of the earlier positions of a game and the comments associated with these positions; the player benefiting from the perspective thus obtained might see trends not obvious from a single view of a board position, while the watcher would better understand the total strategy (or feel of it) when able to study a sequence of positions.

Viewdata is not a replacement for other games, though some are easy to provide. It adds convenience, but most important, it looks like adding capabilities.

8 The electronic diary

Given that a Viewdata user may send messages to other people, can a user send a message to himself? The answer is yes; indeed the message-sending facility has been so arranged in the first Post Office pilot system that it merely checks the identity of the person for whom the message is intended, the only purpose of this check being to help the sender in spotting errors such as incorrect user or destination numbers. However, the system is not concerned if the sender of the message is the same person as the addressee.

Sending messages to oneself — when combined with the facility offered by the system of storing messages for as long as one is prepared to pay the storage charges — opens new application possibilities. Thus a user could have a private storage area in which to enter information he needs to consult frequently. Indeed there is no reason why a user should not also construct his own data base and give it the structure he desires. However, this is not possible using the message facility, since it was not designed for the purpose; message frames can only be accessed in a strict sequential order, last message first, rather than in the structured way in which the information data base is accessed. Moreover, it is not possible to establish pointers from one frame to the next, so that searching more than ten pages or so can be very time consuming.

A much better instrument for building up a private data base is to use the mechanism which Information Providers employ to enter, organise and display their product — the information they sell — utilising the data structuring facilities of the system and limiting access to oneself only or to a nominated group of people in the manner of a closed-user-group. With this arrangement the data base — being private — may be structured in the way most appropriate to the purpose for which it is put together.

It is clear from this discussion that the means are available in Viewdata to provide facilities for users to construct their own data bases for their own purposes. If this development were to be encouraged, what value would it have to the Viewdata user? Clearly much would depend upon the degree of security provided. As private user data is not attached to the main index, the chances are that it will be almost impossible to find without a reference to the starting page. However, this level of security would not be satisfactory, since it would leave one at the mercy of accidental keying or indeed deliberate and systematic searches to discover private information: it would need to be supplemented with the check number facility available to the closed user groups, wherein each page classified under this heading is associated with the user numbers allowed access to it, and a special program checks user identification.

Potential applications

Given then that this level of security is provided for private data bases, what are the potential applications? In the private sector the range of information could include one's own railway time table, shopping list, special items to be on the look-out for such as book lists, record lists, reminders to call on X, telephone numbers, messages received, list of appointments in the days or weeks ahead, birthdays of friends and relatives (particularly wife/husband), expenses incurred and so on. All this is the stuff of which working diaries are made.

But the private data base begins to seem more exciting when

one can associate processing with the stored data. For instance, imagine the value of a reminder program which would scan the stored data periodically and draw attention to the dentist appointment, a clash of meetings, or that most vital and frequently forgotten action — the sending of flowers on one's wife's birthday or wedding anniversary.

What have here been called 'diary facilities' are clearly much more. They are facilities for assembling a private bank of information, from data either personally entered into one's own storage area or else transferred from the public data base to a personal area to await retrieval and manipulation when required.

As authors, we find ourselves in disagreement as to whether the electronic diary will become primarily a professional and/or organisational venture — one in which access will be given as people climb the executive ladder (a replacement for the key to the executive washroom) — or a system used by individuals on their own. SF believes that it will be the first, RM that it will be both. Clearly the way the demand builds will determine whether or not such facilities will be provided on Prestel or just on private systems. However, there is no way of resolving this difference of opinion short of seeing such a system in use and tracking its usage. Since this has yet to happen, the Viewdata electronic diary remains at present solely a possible future system, even if both of us feel that we need it now.

9 Viewdata systems

The one obvious implementation of the system which derives from its generality is in the form of a national utility. However, this is in a way its most difficult implementation, since it has to appear and indeed to operate from the beginning with the full generality it possesses. Had viewdata not originated in the laboratories of the Post Office, it would probably not have been implemented initially on a national scale but rather as a series of individual private systems which — in due course and after much experimentation — might have been joined together to form (or perhaps been replaced by) a public utility.

Nevertheless it is the national utility concept which is the first to be tried out. As a national utility, Viewdata is of great interest to the common carriers who, in most countries, are able to combine the task of information dissemination (or alternatively to provide access to private sources of information) with that of providing communications facilities.

The national implementation of a Viewdata system may be on the model of the UK Prestel system (which we shall call the replicated data base model) and which relies on a multiplicity of mesh-connected or ring-connected Viewdata centres, in each of which is replicated the major part of the data base currently in demand by the local subscribers. Much of this replicated data base is of 'national' interest, i.e. of interest to a large percentage of users, spread geographically over the country. The rest is of interest to local subscribers only and not replicated in other centres, except perhaps in some circumstances — particularly large urban areas — in other centres in the vicinity.

Thus the major part of the information retrieval traffic will be on a local call basis, from a user to the local computer centre, thus achieving the early system design objective of low-cost usage. Only a small percentage of the enquiries will necessitate information being brought either from another Viewdata centre or from a host computer, the home of specialised data bases.

The interconnection of centres and clusters of centres is needed in order to provide for the updating of the data base at regular intervals according to the type of information in store; for the archiving of local and national information to ensure its security and integrity; and for the reconstruction of the information bank at a centre which might have been completely corrupted or accidentally destroyed. Given that such a communications complex must result for the purposes of the maintenance of the data bank and its dissemination, then its off-peak usage for nationwide message communications makes sense in economic and other respects.

Viewdata host model

But there is another possible model of a national Viewdata system. This is the host model. It relies on a small number of data centres in which *all* information is stored — each data centre or host machine specialises in one or more sectors of the total data base — and on a network of Viewdata centres, mesh-connected or ring-connected internally, which act primarily as switching centres in which perhaps only the index pages are stored and to which the users would have access. Here the final data is obtained from the host machines, but only when the user has made a final selection.

Which model is the most appropriate in which circumstances depends on the balance between cost of storage at the Viewdata centres and cost of fetching data from the host centres every time a user demands it, the economic balance depending primarily on how well data communications systems of the packet-switching kind have been developed and the tariffs needed to support them. Available evidence suggests that, given the published tariffs for packet-switching systems in Europe and the US, it is unlikely that the host-model could be as economic as the replicated data base model at the present time, and given the known current trend of communications and storage costs in the next decade, the imbalance can only increase.

Nevertheless, the principle is attractive in the sense that all significant data, and data likely to change frequently, is held at a small number of locations, with adequate protection against accidental damage and corruption being provided, while only the index pages are stored at every Viewdata centre. The storage capacity at these centres could either be reduced drastically or, by maintaining it at the same level (as in a replicated model) the user could find entry points to a much larger data base. Nevertheless the advantages of the replicated data base are currently very substantial, both in terms of cost effectiveness and of security in all its forms.

International applications

At the international level several national systems may be interconnected in a super-mesh. Here Viewdata junctions are nominated as nodes, these nodes acting as international gateways to the respective national centres. In this particular case the international node is not the host machine or even the keeper of the international data bank, but only a switching centre which will direct the traffic to the appropriate national host machine.

This is clearly an entirely different concept in accessing 'rare' information, since one is dealing with a completely different situation in which a user in say Houston, Texas, may require information to be extracted from the national UK data base, e.g. the latest stock exchange prices or even perhaps details of the fishing in some UK local river.

For UK national information, the user in Houston, Texas, will require the complete set of index pages with pointers to tell him in which pages of the London data base (if it is London information which is required) the information will be found. Alternatively he may only require access to the major index classifications, and the act of retrieval might first consist of the fetching of additional index pages from which the final selection is made. The 'response' page process would apply in this case, where a set of index pages is demanded by the user (as when placing an order for the purchase of a product). The system would then process the enquiry by transmitting these pages to the user.

The establishment of Viewdata on a global scale highlights the major problem likely to be encountered in an information retrieval system when the data base become very extensive, whether this occurs at the national or the international level.

The working of a replicated data base system is quite straightforward when the data bases are not too large, a qualification which must be considered in relation to the number of users likely to require access to it. Clearly, a locally held data base is a resource which costs money to maintain and must therefore earn sufficient revenues by being accessed at a known minimum rate to justify its costs.

Given that a Viewdata centre with one 200-port computer can provide access to a total of 0.5 million pages in an 8-hour day; that on the average half the pages will be index pages (because of the need to provide multiple entry points) and the other half data pages; and finally that on the average the annual cost of maintaining a data page is about £20 or approximately 5p per day, including promotion costs; then it follows that a Viewdata distribution centre is economically viable if the *maximum* storage capacity is as follows:

    250,000 pages priced at 1p per page or
    100,000 pages priced at 2½p per page or
    50,000 pages priced at 5p per page or

If the same data is available for access at say twenty centres across the country, then clearly the *maximum* storage capacity at each centre can increase in the same proportion, i.e.:

5,000,000 pages priced at 1p per page or
2,000,000 pages priced at 2½p per page or
1,000,000 pages priced at 5p per page

Adding free pages to the system subtracts from the maximum useful data base size, by at least the same amount, if the assumption implicit made in the above calculation — that all pages are accessed equally — holds. If this assumption does not hold, then the addition of free or low-cost pages could subtract considerably more from the maximum useful size, and by the same token to increase the number of outlets, say from twenty centres to fifty, would increase the maximum useful size of the data base stored at a centre, in the same ratio.

The maximum useful size of a replicated data base cannot be determined as simply as might have been inferred, if only because a database will usually contain a mix of pages with different prices and widely differing appeal. Nevertheless the point to be made is that in a replicated system there is a limit to the useful size of the data base maintained at each centre; hence sooner or later, when the information in demand exceeds that size, it is necessary to rearrange the storage and access system to provide a mix of replicated data bases and host data bases. Host data bases would then be used for the storage of the less frequently required pages, while replicated data bases would be used for those more frequently needed.

The host data base system presents difficult problems of access, as has been seen in the case of the international connection between national systems, where the availability at all centres of the indexes of all the other centres on a global basis is inconceivable, not only because of the massive storage required but also because such a vast data base, almost entirely made up of indexes, is unlikely to be accessed often enough to make it economically viable. An alternative arrangement might consist of using access protocols for international connections, identical to those used for data base access on a local basis, i.e. conduct a dialogue direct with the centre in which the relevant data base is held.

An appropriate example might be that of the user in San Francisco, who wants details of European Arts Festivals so as to plan a European holiday. The San Francisco data base would carry a reference to the location of well-known arts festivals such as Salzburg, Edinburgh etc. Having identified the location of the festival sought, the local Viewdata centre would then act as a switching centre enabling the enquiry to be put directly to the appropriate centre, with which a further dialogue could then be conducted. This would not prevent the local centre in San Francisco from keeping details of the various European Arts Festivals, but this could be based on local demand.

The interconnection of national Viewdata systems on an international basis can only be a long-term objective. It will only come about when a sufficiency of national systems has been established to make their interconnection a useful and profitable exercise. In the meantime, however, the need for extra-national information will be met by establishing special-purpose Viewdata systems intended specifically to fulfill this requirement. A start in this direction has already been made by the UK Post Office which, acting jointly with a consortium of UK Information Providers, is establishing Prestel International, an organisation to deal with international information exchange using Viewdata systems.

Closed user groups

A national system once established will provide a powerful information and communications utility capable of catering for many of the needs of individuals and businesses. Many businesses who otherwise might want to establish their own systems, might prefer to make use of the national system and thus gain the advantage of improved cost-effectiveness, reduced capital outlay and extensive geographical coverage.

These considerations apply to organisations who need to supply information to large numbers of users who may be scattered over a wide geographical area, or even to large numbers of their own staff who are normally situated in widely dispersed geographical locations. To these a nationwide Viewdata system offers new facilities which no other system so far developed can rival: the ability to disseminate information to nominated groups of people at very high speed and very low cost. To this may be added a number of additional facilities such as response pages, which can be designed to be organisation specific. For example, an organisation with broadly based interests covering the whole country needs to make available to its sales force the latest stock position, prices and availability of a wide range of products, and in return requires to know the types of products and quantities sold, deliveries promised, names of customers, prices quoted etc. — information which would normally take several days to assemble, collate and distribute.

With Viewdata this information is not only available to the central sales force but also at the same time to those requiring it in the central planning and managing functions. Furthermore, it is available in the Viewdata computer at the instant of capture and can therefore be transferred to the corporate computers, to fulfil other internal requirements, thus saving much manual effort in the handling of a multiplicity of paper documents throughout the trading cycle (from the initial ordering of the goods to their delivery and the receipt of payments).

There is clearly a security problem involved in that the information relating to the transactions illustrated above must not be accessible to the users of the public Viewdata system. This requirement can be readily satisfied by the closed user group, in which access to a nominated part of the data base is only available to members of a restricted group using a common password for identification. It is also possible to provide considerable added protection to the simple password access code by having a multiplicity of security codes with further identification (by context or signature profile);

however, this is seldom necessary since much of the business transacted, though confidential, does not require extreme security measures.

Where, however, the security needs are of the utmost importance (for example, in the case of military information) a closed user group embedded in a public system is probably not the right vehicle to collect and disseminate information of this nature. A separate system, with a completely independent and self-contained communications network interconnecting machines amongst themselves and users to the machines, is the preferred choice, with as much insulation from the public system as possible.

The concept of the closed user group enables an Information Provider to disseminate confidential information within his organisation or to communicate with a group of specialist business associates. Two types of closed user groups have so far been implemented in Prestel. Closed User Group 1 (CUG 1), allows authorised members to access the information in that group as long as their identity — e.g. user numbers — has been supplied to the system. Closed User Group 2 (CUG 2) is available to all IPs to enable them to temporarily bar users from some of their frames, for instance while the frames are being amended or before the information is complete enough to become 'operational'.

An inverse kind of closed user group, the so-called NULL CUG, allows a terminal to access frames of one or more closed user groups but no other, thus preventing the user of such a terminal from looking at frames outside the closed user groups specified. This facility is clearly useful in certain specialised business applications where the Information Provider sponsoring the user wishes to avoid incurring frames charges for information other than that sponsored. Closed User Groups and their inverse, the NULL CUGs, are two powerful devices designed to expand the marketing of Viewdata beyond the area of public information dissemination. They enable Information Providers to develop a subscription business similiar to that of the specialised newsletter.

A typical CUG of the in-house variety might be used by the

large grocery multiple to provide every one of a thousand branch managers with the latest price changes on every item, advance information on special offers, a list of slow-moving items to promote or indeed any other information which head office requires to be passed on.

A Closed User Group which is more akin to the business newsletter might consist of information relating to marketing data on selected products. One experiment has had to do with bread and bakeries. It provides — amongst other information — a five-year view of the trends in consumption of bread and bakeries in terms of volume and sterling value, the split between the domestic and the catering markets, and the distribution of average household expenditure in terms of pence per head per week between sliced bread, white unsliced bread, brown bread, wholemeal and so on, all information derived from the National Food Survey. Other features of interest beside the overview of the market (i.e. what is the market, what is its size and what are the trends) are the brand pictures within the market and the profiles of the main brands. The illustration shown is culled from the experimental data base and is about Danish King, a brand manufactured by Spillers French. For those in the target group such information in invaluable, not least because of its ready availability, its association with the trend data shown above, and with financial and other related information on the major companies involved in this market area.

An interesting example of a NULL CUG is the one being considered by The New Opportunity Press, specialist publishers of careers and job information for school leavers, graduates and the work-experienced job changer. NOP's publications range from annual encyclopaedic presentations of employers, to more frequent — even fortnightly — vacancy notifications.

For The New Opportunity Press, the constraints imposed by the printed word in dealing with vacancy information were those of timing (a vacancy had to be made known to potential candidates without delay), overloading of the distribution media (schools careers offices and University and Polytechnic careers services tend to be swamped with written notices at certain times); and the problem of notifying changes of circumstances promptly, e.g. to prevent further applications for a vacancy which has already been filled.

With Viewdata most of these constraints could be readily overcome, and vacancies could be entered in the system within hours of notification, the delay depending on the level of demand for the editing services. Once in the system details of vacancies are available to the careers offices instantaneously. Information on posts filled and changed circumstances could equally be disseminated with the same speed. Viewdata also provides a direct correspondence between the published careers manual, giving details of employers and other fairly static material, (distributed free to all UK graduates) and related vacancies which can be found on Viewdata by calling the page number given in the printed publication, thus combining the best that Viewdata and the printed word can provide. The marketing approach to the jobs and career information for graduates consists of supplying careers offices at Universities with Viewdata receivers, on free loan. The use of the NULL CUG facility would limit access to the job pages on Viewdata — thus limiting the charges borne by the Universities to the cost of the local telephone connections to the Viewdata centre.

Thus the CUG concept is developing not only into a medium for instantly disseminating fairly easily perishable information, or information which needs to be acted upon immediately, but also as a repository for comprehensive reference information.

The closed user group concept is an appropriate one for businesses who require Viewdata-like systems for the dissemination of information to a large number of users or customers who are geographically dispersed over a large area, but it is not necessarily valid where the majority of the users are concentrated in one or two principal locations and where the alternative of a stand-alone system might be appropriate.

Already several developments of private Viewdata systems have sprung up in industry and commerce, the main incentives being the ease with which information may be disseminated to the users, the ease with which users are able to access the information they require, and the low-costs compared with other systems of information dissemination. Two private organisations have already announced plans to use Viewdata-like systems for their requirements; one is the UK Stock Exchange, now phasing out their current 2000 terminal Price Display Service which has been in operation in the City since 1969. This provides up-to-the-minute share prices and news, but is now becoming unable to cope with vastly increased information requirements. The system being developed by the Stock Exchange is called TOPIC,* for Teletext Output of Price Information by Computer; it is planned to use the Viewdata concept and method (rather than broadcast Teletext), and will offer up-to-date market prices on up to 1500 securities, plus a more comprehensive news service than is currently available. TOPIC is a true Viewdata system where information is available on demand and only transmitted to the user who requests it, once and once only. TOPIC is also intended to provide a variety of interactive services which a broadcast system cannot offer, and in addition will be capable of connecting up to Prestel, thus providing its user population with access to the Post Office database, and at the same time creating closed user groups within Prestel able to use the specialised data available under TOPIC.

The Whitbread system is by contrast a pilot scheme in operation since early 1978, and used only for the internal dissemination of information. The system, called DAISY (Daily Information System) provides consolidated daily sales and stock statistics for use by the brewery's London-based production managers. It is there to assist them in the planning of production levels for Whitbread's various varieties of beer, at previously located breweries. The system is intended to form the final link in a chain that begins in local offices all over the country, where details of customers' orders for the wide variety of beers and lagers brewed by the Whitbread group are

---

* The TOPIC computers will be MODCOMP Classic 7870s, the specification calling for an ability to respond to over 1000 interrogations every five seconds.

entered in local computers, and then transmitted daily to the five regional computers for further processing. Consolidated figures derived from these systems are transmitted overnight to the central computer in London where final reports are prepared for use the next day. These reports are entered in the DAISY system and displayed on the Viewdata terminals.

The Viewdata terminals have been found to overcome the resistance which many people in industry seem to have to the use of computers. The television set is familiar to everyone, the keypad is as acceptable as the pocket calculator, displays are bright, attractive and legible. The use of colour and graphics provides a number of additional facilities: the ability to highlight important information, the grouping of related data and the display of read-at-a-glance production charts not normally available in computer print-outs. It was not lost on the company that the same terminals could also be used to access the public Viewdata system (for other-than-company information, but information still relevant to their work) and the Teletext services broadcast by the BBC and the IBA.

DAISY has been running with eight Viewdata terminals on the same site, using separate modems, and an extension to eight more terminals at remote sites is at the planning stage.* One of the great advantages of the Viewdata approach for DAISY is the ease of use, the better acceptability of modified TV sets for display purposes, and the conviviality of the computer dialogue. Indeed programmers for DAISY are encouraged to write user-friendly responses, rather than the usual terse, stern and often cryptic phrases of the more conventional information retrieval system.

This centre section has been primarily concerned with the systems currently operating, and how systems can be put together from existing technology. It has shown that some of the technology that exists, however, has not so far been seriously exploited in Viewdata technology. Indeed, one could not expect otherwise, since the technology is still too new.

Though some of the applications we have described are new,

---

* December 1978.

they all have at least one common characteristic — somewhere or other someone is developing or devising them on the basis of the technology we have been describing.

But, as the boy kept on saying in the famous Shelley Berman and Charles Schultz stories, what else is new? You mean that is all there is? Well, no, it is not.

10 The future: section one

Our final section must in some sense be regarded as speculative, itself an understatement. Many of the possible ways in which Viewdata technology will, might and could be used have been described and explored. Almost all have occurred to UK corporate planners and business managers — in industry and in government — in the last two or three years. Some have occurred to us and have been suggested to various managements, with varied degrees of receptivity ranging from outright enthusiasm: 'Why can't I do it now?' to: 'Change the subject.'

Many of the uses we have described are in some form or other (often not that in which the original proposals were made) at some stage of development, the precise stage unfortunately not always being easy to identify, and that usually not only for reasons of commercial secrecy or confidentiality. Though the triad of allies, the PO/PTTs, the information providers and the set manufacturers, are a unique combination in bringing the technology/service to the market, the newness of the alliance is itself limiting. The joint development of a technology by separate and disparate industries with differing traditions, different ways of doing business and initially different aims can be quite difficult when there is no central driving force which can instruct everybody to do *this* and in *that* time scale and expect to be obeyed.

Viewdata may look like a homogeneous technology, but it does not have a homogenous organisation behind it. Its generality and spread across many industries may mean that in the long term it becomes a major media, however in the short term....

Hence, though Viewdata has been received with great enthusiasm by most of those who have been exposed to it, both in the UK and abroad, and progress may be more than in the eye of the beholder, it does not have the clear clean shape of progress in a technology under the control of one single source, one supplier, one view of the market, and an organisation geared to that view and that view alone.

We have laboured this point at length for the good and sufficient reason that it is impossible to take a firm definite view of Viewdata technology and to state that by such and such a date the sweep of services we have described will be available on the market, either in the UK or elsewhere, and that this is what the market will then look like.

The reasons for our inability to give firm fixed estimates are many. For a start market tests, trials, experiments and a limited public service may give some idea of user reactions; user profiles, however, are something else, and depend on having fixed regular services at known prices. As yet, one can only say that though we foresee millions of users, a great mass public market 'out there' which needs the information that can be offered on Prestel/Viewdata, nobody is absolutely sure how it will react until the services are actually offered. We still have to operate by 'gut feel' in many ways.

Next, we come to the question of technology and the planning cycle. The problem is that each organisation involved has its own norms, so that there is no overal norm. Moreover, if there is no norm in one society, there is even less likely to be a norm across many: cultural, social and economic differences preclude it.

Even if there were to be a norm within one society, and it was possible to state that the totality of the services described would be available by 1985 or 1990, this still would not give an all-inclusive picture of the technology and the market at either date. For at the time of writing both are sufficiently far away in time for new entrants to come in, perhaps in force, entrants who as yet have no idea that they will be in the Viewdata market place.

It may well be that their entrance in turn will depend on the pace at which both technology and market develop. We are here in the world of second, third and fourth order preferences, and any authors with a sense of prudence would be best advised to state that these are the problems and pass quickly on.

All we can then do is to give our personal estimate of how the technology and market are likely to develop.

The strategy concepts and possibilities

The current round of interest in Viewdata is concerned with concepts and possibilities, and with an embryo first-stage working technology. Almost everywhere you look, the initial providers have made a reservation of frames sufficient to enable them to run meaningful tests, are putting up one database (and sometimes experimenting with others) and — tucked away in their business/commercial development departments, where they have them — are trying to work out what to do next. Paper studies abound: indeed a check around a number of database providers in the summer of 1978* indicated that for every database to which they have some sort of commitment or which has actually been seen, there may well be four to five others at some stage of consideration.

Translating this into commercial reality then is somewhat difficult, and is made more so by two critical dependencies over which the information providers have little control. Both are UK Post Office bound and have to do with its Prestel service. Externally, that service is the model which

---

* The situation in mid-1979 was considerably improved, with substantial data bases in existence, the total number of pages in that use amounting to 122,000 on 22 June 1979.

organisations, particularly telecommunications suppliers, are using to evaluate Viewdata. They may have plans, but the PO is gathering installation experience, and there is a tendency to test assumptions against the development record of Prestel. Internally in the UK that experience both expands and limits the way the market develops.

The two dependencies are the PO learning curve, and its effect on service provision and the charging levels it will (or may) set for the public service. Though these two are inextricably intertwined, nevertheless some disentanglement is possible.

The problem is that the correct strategy to follow in the development of Prestel is far from clear. The Prestel management is venturing into completely new territory and so far lacks the resources to handle and control Viewdata at the rate at which it is developing; in a sense they are the victims of too much enthusiasm. The trouble with generality, with a system which can fill as many requirements as there are points of view, is that those requirements cannot all be filled at once. This is not a new situation. In the early days of computer time-sharing, a number of companies considering entry into the field often made the error of going out and asking potential customers what kind of service they would like to have, given the new technical capability. The answers were of course predictable: everybody had a different idea, and where the ideas were similar the requirements put forward were usually incompatible. The result was that the companies set out to create large systems which would be all things to all men, and predictably often ended up by offering very little to any of them.

The error was seen and the mistakes corrected, but not before the market's expectations had been blown up out of all proportion to immediately realisable reality, and many would-be users and customers had turned away. As for the successful providers, they started in a small way, devising methods which would have a substantial market, and then going out and offering whatever they had.

Equally important in the Prestel case is another problem

with generality. Prestel also has generality within the Post Office. It does not come to market with its own facilities, under its own control, solely installed by Prestel staff, but is dependent for facilities on other parts of the PO. It is also dependent on a telecommunications technology which is changing, and an investment plan outside Prestel management's control. This is so in switching technology, line provision, even the development of the computers and the storage media. And of course the installation of the junction box, the critical user link, will be handled by the same installation engineers who instal and service phones.

Hence the learning curve — for the PO as a Prestel provider, and for the users — is likely to be not at all smooth. The learning curve however is also concerned with other factors besides the tuning of the PO's organisation, factors which might not seem immediately apparent as being inbuilt to that curve at all, yet which if Prestel Viewdata flies fast may well cause considerable short-term problems.

Now it would be pleasant if Prestel Viewdata were to be installed nationwide over a weekend, complete with network transfer arrangements so that if one computer system is fully loaded, load shedding can take place without the user being aware that the system with which they are in communication is not in fact the local one but may be perhaps a hundred miles away.

However, it will not be installed in this way. The initial systems are individual, hence if the local Viewdata system is engaged that is the signal the would-be user will receive.

Now Prestel Viewdata was initially devised for use over standard telephone circuits, switched by conventional electromechanical exchanges, though economically it should be better suited to a digital transmission system, the system that the PO is bringing in. But that system will not blanket the UK till at the earliest the late 1980s, and more probably it will be the early 1990s.

So digital transmission is not what Prestel will initially run on nationwide. As is well known, the telephone exchanges currently used by the Post Office have been installed on the basis of certain traffic expectations, a pattern of usage derived from statistical data dealing with the length of the average phone call which have been arrived at over many years.

However, Prestel Viewdata's usage patterns are at present an unknown quantity; all we know is that we expect them to be different. What is more, Prestel's implementation is coming about sooner rather than later. Initially no one foresaw a problem here. The Post Office was expected to go forward at its usual steady pace, and the industrial reaction to Viewdata was not expected to be as enthusiastic as it has proved.

Now if the Post Office is right, if Prestel Viewdata takes off on the business market before the home market, with high usage rates first noticeable *before* cheap telephone hours, the possibility arises of blocked exchanges and users unable to get through. (Although digital services might be expected to make a difference, both economic and to levels of service, in practice in the initial years this is unlikely to be so.)

All this should not prove a major problem over the long haul: certainly most of the problems are susceptible to solutions either of technology or of volumes — more exchanges, more lines, more connections and so on. Even so the effect of the horrors to come will no doubt have an impact on the development of the public market, which in turn could impact on the rate at which the numbers of sets in use increase — or not. The consequences are impossible to foresee.

These are unlikely to be the only learning curve problems that the Post Office will face, yet even so the list is enough to go on with. However, it is not only the Post Office which faces problems of this order; they will affect — indeed already are affecting — the other two groups: the set manufacturers and the Information Providers.

Problems

The set manufacturers have to contend with a situation in which the technological changes they incorporate into their product become of two kinds. One kind is familiar: the normal processes of technical change in components and their costs dedicated to the same usual end, the production of an improved television receiver able to give in turn better picture/sound quality. Here they have already been undergoing substantial change as they replace discrete components with integrated circuits. The second kind of change however is not so familiar. The model changes that Viewdata make possible are not simply of the kind above, but are also changes in function — extension in the capability of the receiver turning an analogue system into one that is also digital and computer based. Here the managements of the television manufacturers generally lack experience; and one could hardly expect the situation to be otherwise.

The problems faced by the second group, the IPs, are concerned with the creation of the services they seek to offer. Because of the generality of Viewdata technology (about which much has been written in these pages) it is often quite easy to derive a possible data base or service from the Viewdata concept. However, it is not often quite as easy to turn that concept into a commercial offering, nor necessarily as inexpensive as might at first glance be thought.

Here of course there is no generality to the rule. Some organisations will be able to put up databases at much less cost than others: it would seem that those already in the business of data preparation — the publishing companies, particularly journal and newspaper publishers with already-existing in-house staff manning keyboards and telephones (classified advertisement gathering and preparation departments for instance) — should have an economic edge. We suspect that edge will be even greater where they have design departments capable of transferring their skills to the design of Viewdata frames. The others will have to go elsewhere for both services, the first of which in the summer of 1978 were already available at between £4 and £20 per frame.

The first group too should have a quicker reaction time, and that may well give them a substantial marketing edge. There is as yet little experience of the dynamics of Viewdata services, the rate of frame change likely to be required to provide a service upon which the user relies, and to which he returns again and again. The rates, too, will differ: the updating of an encyclopaedia for instance may well be irregular, with some subjects remaining almost unchanged from one year to the next, while others (where variation in subject content is frequent) require changes as frequently as once a week or more. An example of the first group with an encyclopaedia would be, say, a well documented aspect of history in which most of the research has been done over many years, and where additions to knowledge are consequently unlikely to be frequent. An example of the second group would be one concerned with advances in solid-state physics, where new papers seem to appear at least once a week, sometimes it feels almost daily.

It is true that there is some experience in the field of advertising, yet here again one cannot be certain that the experience will transfer directly to Viewdata. This in turn depends on whether the organisations offering the advertising databases structure them in the same way as they structure those they offer in the conventional print media. As already stated, Viewdata does offer new possibilities, grouping by price and locale which run contrary to normal practice in, for instance, daily UK national Press advertising columns.

There are also going to be problems of design. Many of the initial databases show little evidence of a sense of visual design *related to Viewdata*. They could not be expected to for the frame presents opportunities and imposes constraints new to most designers; forty columns, seven colours with no shading opportunities, restrictions on curves, hidden control characters — which can bring a separation between colours and characters not in the designer's original — are not restrictions of which most have much experience. Indeed, initially the notion that visual designers would be a necessity was mainly unappreciated by those considering putting up databases, the few exceptions mostly coming from people with some expertise in presenting educational materials — people who regarded Viewdata not as another medium to which existing services could be transferred but as a new medium in its own right where the design ground rules established over the years for other media did not apply.

However, one way or another the learning curve problem at least for some will come to an end, as such curves do: in this Viewdata should be no different.

Pricing Prestel-Viewdata

Next we come to the charging problem, a problem of a different order. We do not in fact believe that other media have the relevance to Viewdata that the conventional wisdom assumes. The reason is simple: one may begin by thinking of a new medium as a substitute for others, initially using it to handle extracts, versions, re-writes of data originally created for other media. What has been quite clear in the past, and we see no reason why Viewdata should be different, is that a new medium makes its own rules for itself as it goes along. And those rules may have little relevance to those found in other and prior media.

Neither do we believe that the volume usage dependence of Viewdata is at all well understood. The cost characteristics were inbuilt into Viewdata from the start: the nearest comparison we can find — one where a charge is actually made directly — is not with another media but with the products of the integrated circuit — i/c — industry, products which can have a high initial cost which is volume independent, and an infinitesimally low (indeed almost trivial) production/ marketing cost thereafter.

It is noticeable within that industry that pricing, being volume sensitive, which is something well understood, leads to intensive marketing. It is noticeable too that the i/c industry, when faced with competition, cuts prices sometimes dramatically: it can do so because the industry has an in-built awareness of the transient nature of its products.

Unfortunately Viewdata is not the i/c business from day one.

Though Viewdata may be different, it is not however being initially marketed as if it were. This is in some ways understandable. Though the analogues to go by may be unreliable, being largely transfers of experience from other media, yet assumptions are being built in which would indicate that those analogues are being relied on.

So Prestel-Viewdata is being launched as a relatively high price service, an error of considerable magnitude which we can illustrate quite easily.

A local telephone call after six pm gives twelve minutes for three pence. The PO's proposed charges as of the summer of 1979 were for a connect charge to Prestel-Viewdata of a further one pence per minute, plus the IP charge: the one pence per minute charge was based on the notion that a user would access four frames a minute — we write 'notion' because there is no evidence on which to base such a proposition. On this basis, and allowing say for a minimum IP charge per frame of half one pence, a four-frame search carried out in the minimum time would cost an average of about 3½ pence.

Our book has been full of searches at this level, though we have not put such a time restriction upon them. Suppose, for arguments' sake, one such call per day per subscriber, or ninety calls a quarter. This seems a reasonable start, though as Prestel-Viewdata encourages browsing it is unlikely to remain a constant across all subscribers.

Nevertheless, let us proceed as if it *were*. We are now considering an extra £3.15 a quarter on top of the quarterly phone bill (which includes £1 a quarter rental charge for the Prestel-Viewdata junction box connection to the phone line) or £12.60 a year. This is about one quarter of the annual cost of taking a daily paper such as *The Times* or the *Guardian*, once a day, six days a week, for a year. But there is also the extra rental to be paid for the hire of the television set. During the market trials, the industry has been hiring sets out at a rental of £18 a month, which is considerably more than the average rental for a non-Viewdata television receiver (in fact, more than twice as much as one of us currently pays). It would not be unfair to state that at this time, the economics of Prestel-

Viewdata as given create a problem. Were the figures we have outlined to be considered realistic (at 1978 prices), then all Prestel-Viewdata market forecasts would in turn seem rather unrealistic. So what is going to give?*

For a start, the equipment rental may come down and that quite quickly. The reason takes us back to Chapter 1: the unwillingness of many manufacturers to let the market once more go to the rental companies. In the middle of 1978, there is talk within the industry of sets being on the market at prices equivalent to standard colour televisions within two to three years. Allowing for inflation, one can foresee sets on the rental market which add little more than 20 per cent to the existing rental bill by that time.

---

* The PO charging structure has changed as of the Summer 1979:

Prestel costs: After 6pm and at week ends

1 Connect time mins	2 Phone cost	3 Prestel cost	4 Info cost 0.5p/p	5 Cost of session	6 Cost per min	7 Cost of session no info cost: free pages 0.0p/p	8 Cost per min
1	3	3	2	8	8	6	6
2	3	3	4	10	5	6	3
3	3	3	6	12	4	6	2
4	3	6	8	17	4.25	9	2.25
5	3	6	10	19	3.80	9	1.80
6	3	6	12	21	3.50	9	1.50
7	3	9	14	26	3.71	12	1.71
8	3	9	16	28	3.50	12	1.50
9	3	9	18	30	3.33	12	1.33
10	3	12	20	35	3.50	15	1.50
11	3	12	22	37	3.36	15	1.36
12	3	12	24	39	3.25	15	1.25

For information charges of 0.5p per page cost of using Prestel varies from 8p per minute for very short sessions to 3.25 per minute for the longer sessions.
For free information pages cost per minute vary between 6p per minute and 1.25p per minute.
A fair assessment is to take the average cost of a 6 minute session as representative of the cost per minute of using Prestel. Average is ½(3.50 + 1.50) = 2.5p per minute.

Thus, while the PO and IP charges may appear reasonable for very limited usage, an average of 6 minutes per day, they will both need to come down substantially to compete with other media, if a habit and a profitable market are to be built up. For if they do not, they will in turn impact on the growth of the very market that the Post Office is initially intending to spend £100 million developing.

So far, this chapter has been concerned with caution, with the gap between expectation in the short term and the problems of a likely reality. That we have been able to write this before the event, even if more problems arise than we have discussed, is itself of interest: it indicates that the problems are susceptible to a solution. This is the way expertise is built up, and experience gained.

We estimate that by 1981-2, in the UK at least, most of the problems described will have been gone through (and fought through, whether in public or private) by enough organisations, set manufacturers, IPs, the Post Office and users for there to be a substantial revenue base and a rapidly developing market beginning to show some clear characteristics.

Therefore it is from that perspective, that we now turn to the Viewdata revolution proper, for by that time the conditions for such a revolution will be present. We now intend to examine the dimensions of that revolution, and we start with a Prestel Viewdata receiver scenario for the eighties which makes a useful frame for discussion.

Table A Rate Forecast: UK Households Television receivers equipped to receive Prestel Viewdata

A)	1981	1982	1983	1984	1985	1986	1987	1988	1989	1990
%	1/1½	3/4	7/8	17/23	32/38	45/59	50/55	55/60	60/65	67/70

Table A* gives our estimates of the set population in the UK by households through the 1980s. It allows for a slower start-up, *pace* the views put forward in the last twenty or thirty paragraphs, than the euphoric discussion of Viewdata in the media in 1977/8 would imply. In terms of numbers the figures are shown in Table B.

Table B1 Forecast: Total number of Prestel Viewdata equipped receivers installed in the UK. In numbers (millions).

1981	1982	1983	1984	1985	1986	1987	1988	1989	1990
.25	.7	1.3	4.0	6.5	8.5	9.4	10.2	11.0	12.0

Table B2 Forecast: Prestel Viewdata equipped receivers delivered to UK market (Millions)

.18	.45	.6	2.7	2.7	2.5	2.3	2.3	2.5	2.5

(1978 Post Office Forecasts assume 3 million sets installed by 1983, half a million of them in businesses. We believe that the learning curve problems outlined will delay arriving at these figures by 18 months, possibly two years.)

These figures are subject to the usual statistical disclaimer: a variation of 10-20 per cent, that variation being looser the further away we move in time. The qualifications have to be made if the exercise is not to lose touch with reality.

We believe that these projections do not so lose touch. If the reader accepts this, then one of the reasons why the UK television industry has latched on to Viewdata becomes apparent. The 1977 Abstract of Statistics (CSO) shows colour television production for the years 1973 through 1976 as falling from a production peak of 2.12 million to 1.54 million. During the same period monochrome set production also fell: from 1.01 million to 0.56 of a million (since when both have fallen even further).

A further dependency has to do with receiver variants, availability and price. The assumption is that a standard

---

* The figures in Tables A, B1 and B2 are based on a synthesis of the results of private discussions with executives in the television receiver manufacturing industry. The estimates have dependencies: they assume that by 1983 the state of Prestel service will be such that there will be complete UK national coverage, that the databases will have been sufficiently developed as to give a wide variety of services also available nationally, and that Prestel services will be actively marketed by the triad.

Viewdata-equipped receiver, complete with decoder/modem and numeric/control keypad, will be available at the same retail price by 1982-3, as a non-Viewdata-equipped colour receiver of comparable size; also that sets offering enhanced capability — full alphanumeric keyboard and/or local storage — will be available as a standard consumer product (though at a premium) by the same date.

It will be noted that the sharp rise in Prestel-Viewdata-equipped households comes roughly ten to eleven years after the last colour television sales 'boom', and the assumption has been made that those receivers will be replaced by sets equipped for Prestel-Viewdata.

One further assumption is that some form of message service will be on offer by the PO in 1980-1 at the latest, and that this will — probably in extended form — give national coverage and be available as a matter of routine in 1984.
continuation of this chapter.

As the estimates — Table B — show, we have industry sales to the UK market at one and a half to two million sets a year from 1984 through 1986, though we make no forecasts as to where those sets will come from. However, assuming price stability — a large, though possible, assumption because of changes in components and their costs — say a retail value of £450 (averaged) for a Viewdata receiver, we could be contemplating an annual UK retail market of £900 million through this period. The second set of figures in Table B do not match the first; the reason for this is that we have reduced Viewdata television receiver life from nine to five/six years, in line with the model changes that we expect to see.

Thus the first line would give rough estimates of UK sales through to 1990, assuming that Viewdata could be marketed on the basis of a fully operational 'Mark One' service: on the same basis as if Viewdata sets were television sets and with no replacement. Line B2 however assumes that alphanumeric keyboards will be standard and that the message/electronic mail service begins in 1983-4; that there is a learning curve here as in the initial start-up years (which will also bring its crop of horrors); and that the initial Viewdata sets start to be replaced by new models with more facilities around 1984. It assumes also that 'normal' television sets are replaced by Viewdata sets. No assumptions have been made as to the penetration of Viewdata into the business market, which could have an effect on the figures. Neither are these figures meant to be taken as production figures for the UK industry. Because much of the current push is being made by ITT and Thorn, it may well be that production will be spread out on a European basis. Nor has the riposte of the Japanese industry been taken into account, hence some of the sets may well be manufactured outside Europe.

The reader will note that we have assumed market stabilisation in the UK in the mid- to late eighties: from 1986 onwards, growth is steady. This is a view of the market situation in the UK, and it should not be read as a view of UK set production. We do expect that by the mid-eighties a substantial export business will be developing.

It is obvious that the further into the late eighties we go, the less reliable the figures become. Hence some clarification is in order. We believe that these figures are easily realisable on the basis of a scenario in which the market, facilities, sets and services all march in step, even if only roughly so. Indeed the scenario is conservative: were there to be little more change than we have outlined in these pages, this is the way the consensus — as of autumn 1978 — indicates that the market would develop.

Can these 'forecasts' be 'fleshed' out? We believe so. What follows is a different scenario, year by year into the late eighties, indicating some of the developments we expect might or could happen, and some of their consequence.

---

* As of late Spring 1979, when the final manuscript was being revised, the view that installation would run late was being borne out. Public manufacturing industry forecasts assumed a set population in the UK by end of 1980 still below 100 000.

11 The future: section two

1980

Post Office Prestel Viewdata public service began in 1979 and ran late from day one, indeed day one should have been around day ninety. However, Prestel computer centres are now up and working in London, Manchester, Birmingham, with extensions to Bristol and Norwich. At the start of the year Prestel has up only about a quarter of a million usable pages, many data bases still being very experimental. There are now between 120 and 150 suppliers of pages with material actually on the system, of whom only twenty to thirty can be counted as serious — in terms of volumes (1500 frames or more).

Post Office has installation problems, both with computers within the network and junctions boxes in user premises. Problems abound, for the good and varied reasons given in the first part of this chapter, and calls are heard for the reshaping of Viewdata management, services and pricing. Whether or not this is deserved is subsumed in the resultant public fuss. The situation is complicated by political problems as the argument over the possible break-up of the Post Office continues, with further complications arising from the inevitable party political character of the responses.

Tentative start made with business systems on the market which are data-structure and operating-software compatible with Prestel, allowing private systems to be built and installed, with cross links to the public system. First business systems used by large companies and organisations — not, as the optimists would wish, the smaller ones. Closed user groups begin based on commercial commonality, the basis being straightforward information retrieval.

Prestel expanded to give cover of all the larger urban areas in the UK. Networking problems arise. Fall-out begins as some information providers find that the databases they have put up are not attracting a user market, for reasons which have to do both with lack of terminal population and lack of initial thought about the nature of the media and the type of database that might be useful. Database development continues, with emphasis on large encyclopaedic databases, though no one expects more than a few of these to surface for a long time. Data entry problems become prominent, as do data entry costs, and some people are heard saying, 'We can't go on like this.'

Post Office rejigs the charging structure for the second time.

Access charges fall, and promises are made that they will fall further as market expands.

Unexpectedly, the business market is not the one that was generally foreseen, but rather the transfer of existing database systems into Viewdata format, which are then accessed and displayed on Viewdata terminals. First Viewdata terminal with built-in tape recorder, and Viewdata attachable small printers reach the business market.

Closed user groups expand: first tentative experiments of EFTS with real transactions but not on a public access basis, limited to banks and groups of customers: travel trade and major stores, and dealing initially with credit card transactions.

It transpires that you do not need a Viewdata set to receive Prestel. Two manufacturers of personal computers — now selling at anything from £300 to £1000 — of which there are getting on for 60000-80000 installed in the UK, announce Post Office approved Prestel interfaces. Plug in to your desk top computer and into the phone jack, and away you go.

1981

Prestel coverage continues to expand. Post Office finds that usage is not high enough, active Post Office marketing ensues. Charging structure rejigged once more. Post Office announces that the programming provision service in which more than information retrieval is possible — a development under consideration for four years and on which program IPs have been working for even longer — commences on a limited basis, as does message service for the disabled. Rash of announcements by IPs offering games, education services and conventional programming facilities.

Large databases begin to pick up. Volumes now high enough in limited areas for statistical studies to show how Viewdata is developing and the types of data that people are finding useful. Studies show that on the public service, the saddle effect is working, closely paralleling prior developments in computing: people seek highly specific databases, or go to browse in the very large generalised databases. Cross linkage indexing facilities become the rage, and many different schemes are considered, none of which look very satisfactory. Situation is not resolved because people are looking for a generality in these schemes, and there are always exceptions leading to complexity.

Business systems market continues to grow. Viewdata systems now available also on mini-computers with floppy discs for storage as a matter of course. Attack begins on the retail market, offering initially on-line stock control. Viewdata making inroads into small business systems market, but being used primarily by sophisticated still quite large companies for such items as individual project control.

Closed user groups: roughly the same as before, but a year of expansion.

1982

Post Office announces that by sometime next year, full national coverage will be possible. The message transmission experiments it has been conducting since 1974 will now allow for a limited public message service this year.

Cross-linking to Telex begins on a limited basis. Initial service restricted to major cities with Viewdata exchanges. This recognises an embarassing reality: the skilled have been using Viewdata technology for message transmission since 1978, and a sort of bootleg telex system is already growing up.

The services are aimed at different markets: Viewdata-Telex at business, the message service at the home. Initially the message service will not encompass the split-screen conversational facility as in the service for the deaf, but will be limited to messages of the greetings card type. Such service also to begin on a limited international basis to West Germany, Holland and the USA, with the additional twist that the service is further cross-linked to the existing international telegram service so that telegrams can be initiated by Viewdata.

Access to European databases to be also available via Prestel and Euronet.

The hobbyist computer experiments with Viewdata carried on since 1978, in which attempts are made to integrate a microprocesor into Viewdata receivers, are given the PO imprimatur. Its joint microprocessor standards committee with industry having finalised standards the previous year, the first intelligent Viewdata terminals appear on the mass market. They allow for limited local processing and two-way interaction through the embryo programming service. Initial ordering is heavy, but mainly from within the computer industry and education areas.

An unexpected effect of Prestel Viewdata — at least unexpected by the Post Office — is the destruction of the home telephone answering machine business. When Prestel began, such machines were available on a minimum of a three-year rental, at around £150 a year. (In that different society, the USA, the removal of restrictions on the equipment that can be attached to a telephone line, and the ability to purchase telephone answering machines, has brought their price down to where (1978) such a machine could be bought (not rented) for £45, or a tenth of the three-year British rental.)

The party is over: the store-and-forward capability of Prestel Viewdata makes it possible to do without. Cards and letter heads are now being printed carrying phrases to the effect that if there is no answer, leave a message on Prestel, and we will call you back. The Post Office, making the best of it, starts advertising accordingly. After all, it is another way of selling more Post Office service.

The Post Office also announce that Prestel is eventually to go packet switched. It became apparent to the Post Office and the PTTs in the mid-seventies that packet switching was ideally suited to the short message or enquiry. By the late seventies Post Office spokesmen were talking of a split in technologies, with packet switching being the way of communicating over the network for short messages, while bulk traffic and long connections continue essentially over circuit-switched parts of the network. The network has been developing accordingly.

So why should not the split also happen at the local telephone end? Of course, this will mean that Viewdata terminals will require some local intelligence, if the user is not to have to tie up the line, pumping down one character after another, which would defeat the object of the exercise.

However, this now means that as packet switching will take some time to introduce nationwide, two standards will prevail throughout most of the eighties.

Packet-switched terminals, states the Post Office, will face communications charges arrived at on a totally different basis: the Post Office after all wishes to speed up conversion. A simple four-level enquiry call would involve communications costs of a penny a call.

This seemingly astounding price drop is not found to be quite as radical as at first appeared. Prestel is being used, it transpires, in different ways from those initially envisaged. There are a preponderance of calls averaging three or four searches into a database, each search going down to six or seven levels, incurring communications charges longer than the minimum. Instead of user telecommunications charges decreasing, the increase is of the order of 15 per cent.

Business systems market expands: particularly noticeable is the emerging offer of closed user group facilities aimed at businesses, mostly directed at systems to be delivered in the next two years. These include sales services: Viewdata has saved the salesman from having to take a computer terminal around with him to link into his own company's unique computer system. He can now use the Viewdata terminal in his customer's premises, dialling up his own company's system, and obtaining confirmation of availability, price, delivery date and so on in the presence of the customer.

Public Prestel system comes into operation, initially at airports and railway stations. The sets can take either cash or the experimental magnetic cash card the Post Office announced in 1978, with the card being directly debited by the system as it is used. However, the sets are promptly vandalised, causing MPs of all parties to wax wroth and take up acres of Hansard.

The social consequences of Viewdata are now seen to be a subject of concern, worry, interest etc., according to point of view. Working parties are set up and pronouncements made by government, the NCCL, the TUC. A charitable body points out that Viewdata is another of these systems which discriminates against those socially disadvantaged, the people who cannot read. What is more, the proliferation of the use of colour in the organisation of Viewdata frames to make essential points also discriminates against the colour-blind.

Comments are made that the UK is falling behind in Viewdata technology. Many of the new ideas are coming from abroad, particularly the USA, which after sorting out the problems caused by the separation between computing and telecommunications — which had precluded the telephone companies from offering Viewdata-like services — has latched on to Viewdata and is moving ahead quite rapidly.

A demonstration of Viewdata systems is given to the Cabinet, showing some of the uses to which government departments are putting Viewdata technology. The receiver fails: a loose plug connection.

1983

Full national coverage achieved, intensive Post Office and IP promotion. Bottlenecks in receiver production, causing frustration to users: sets with in-built micros, tape recorders, printers and alphanumeric keyboards now available — if you can get them.

The Post Office announces that the conversational facility will be available from next year. Objections by some — but not all — unions.

Post Office also announces a batch facility for overnight mail, in conjunction with software and systems houses who will work on adapting existing in-house computing systems. Meanwhile Post Office will continue work on development of a next generation Viewdata system.

Market characteristics looking clearer. Though national coverage is in practice limited, some patterns are beginning to emerge. Socially it would be desirable if Prestel Viewdata were to provide an information resource in country and thinly populated areas. In fact Prestel is largely city bound, with more than half the sets in use in the South East, 40 per cent of them being in London. Usage begins to show clear-cut patterns: executives have a set at home as well as at the office, but Viewdata has not broken into the middle-class home market in the way that was initially expected. Instead the market is primarily working class, and heavily concentrated on goods and services for sale, and educational material. The middle-class market shows signs of opening up, but is largely concerned with message services and with calculations requiring the programming service. In business, Viewdata systems are beginning to be seen to be (temporarily) limited. What is required is a screen which has better resolution and 80 characters for full business correspondence. However, following the early educational experiments, it is now being seen that Viewdata is a good vehicle for programmed instruction, and a market accordingly develops.

This is the year of the small stand-alone Viewdata system: such systems are on offer to small traders, they are public

Prestel Viewdata compatible, but come with a cassette tape library of accounting and other packages.

Meanwhile the message facility is causing problems: (it is a hot summer). The problems of form filling increase. So why should not the Administration begin to make enquiries from businesses and individuals via Prestel, such enquiries being responded to also via Prestel. Predictable furore, and cries of, 'Big Brother was not supposed to be here till next year.'

In the field of closed user groups, first experiments carried out in commercially polling a closed community, the doctors. Move made by pharmaceutical manufacturer testing new drug who obtained address listings through public channels. More furore on lines above, and enquiry announced.

1984

By now the PO's investment is paying off, even though when the sums are done it is seen that the forecast £100 million investment has so far become £300 million. However Prestel Viewdata is seen to be one of the least labour-intensive systems ever devised. The installation rate, which has been fluctuating not only because the industry cannot deliver (and the gap cannot be filled by the Japanese) but also because of installation problems which seem to come once every six months, have still made it possible to cover over 20 per cent of all households. The saddle effect continues to exert a pull on the way the market is developing, but that is expected to weaken. There is now an added twist: up market, the executive classes are finding it essential to have two television sets since the time when they wish to use Prestel Viewdata at home is often the time when there is family viewing.

The two-television set home is becoming the two-Viewdata set home. However, initially this is not affecting the size of the colour-set market: the majority of second sets being installed seem to be black and white with full keyboard, refined versions of the sets produced as far back as 1978 by GEC, STC etc.

The year is one of excitement: the talk in Viewdata circles is of half the country being linked into Prestel within two years.

Viewdata is rapidly becoming part of the scenery, with some predictable effects as expected. The first case has come before the Social Security Commissioners: is Viewdata a necessity, one to be paid for by the Department? The case concerns an unemployed teacher, supporting an aged relative and currently taking an Open University course (the Open University switched to Viewdata terminals in 1980 and there has since been a substantial increase in its on-line services).

The Commissioners — taking the same view as their counterparts in California with cars, refrigerators and telephones — give a qualified 'yes', though their findings indicate that each case will be judged on its merits. There is a predictable outcry with MPs popping up and down from the back benches questioning the Minister responsible.

The row sputters out in ten days, only to start up again when a press release from the Manpower Services Training Agency announces a set of Prestel training modules aimed at the unemployed. Does this mean that Viewdata systems are now going to be parcelled out to all and sundry? It does not: but no one listens to the answer.

The Post Office is now feeling confident, but this is only at the operational level, though even there local twists on Viewdata are beginning to cause problems. There are those who maintain that specific frames in parts of the Viewdata service give — in anagram form — the answers to the problem of who killed President Kennedy; spell out F . . . and other obscene comments; and that if you read for example the first letter in each line in frame ... this will always give you the result of the 2.30 at Windsor or wherever. Amateur comedians catch on and put in obscene jokes, using the first letter of words in specific frames, and the word spreads as the word does.

This has the effect of overloading some exchanges. All these questions of course now become policy questions, and rows ensue with the Advertising Standards Authority and the Church holding a watching and intervening brief.

More seriously, Viewdata is beginning to have a serious

impact on television advertising. The chairman of the independent television company who remarked in 1978 that 'he needed Teletext like he needed a hole in the head' is seeing his worst fears realised, though it is his successors who are faced with the problem of working out what to do about it.

They have done quite well with Viewdata until now. Television advertisements carrying, 'Dial up Prestel Frames...' captions are a financially rewarding business, even if they have had to be limited to the last advertisement in any segment because of protests by other advertisers. It has meant that some viewers have missed part of a transmission, but since all they seem to have lost is a part of the programme segment and not the advertising, the companies have not been too disturbed.

However, evidence is now beginning to appear of lower viewing figures generally, which affect the ratings and thus advertising revenues. The trouble is not simply caused by Prestel, but also by the other uses to which Viewdata terminals can be put. The inbuilt cassette and the ability to run tapes locally have brought the games purveyors out in full swing. For instance, you can play Monopoly on- or off-line with an intelligent Viewdata receiver. Star Wars games are now considered old hat. Viewdata is even being used as moving wallpaper. A cassette graphics generator which draws pretty and abstract pictures is the latest craze: it seems to have some psychadelic effects. Prestel banned its transmission, but this has not stopped cassette sales.

What Prestel has not banned is a home movie by wire delivery service. Video home recording has been increasing in importance in parallel to Viewdata, and home libraries are being built up. It seems obvious that the intelligent Viewdata terminal and the telephone line between them can be put to other uses. Can the new facility be used to deliver films by landline? It can, but the line time used will be inordinate. To digitise a film and send it down a normal telephone line could take about ten times as long as the film's running time. However, the Post Office has begun to install fibre optics connections for some new phones, and here there is little disparity. A company announces 'films by wire'. The Post

Office welcome it and propose assistance: after all, whichever way it is done, it is going to eat up line time which the user will have to pay for.

Of course, if the UK were considering a national satellite service, with individual dish aerials for those who wish them, or local dish aerials and fibre optic connections to households, there would be few problems. However, no such national system is in the offing, though it was suggested as far back as the late 1960s.

It being 1984, you can be certain that anything which *can* be related to George Orwell's book *will* be so related. First, design details of the new Post Office terminals are leaked. Though this terminal was foreseen in 1978, the usual figures in the TUC, the CBI and politics indicate that it is unlikely to be of serious public concern in their lifetimes. Now it transpires that the Post Office and the Gas and Electricity Boards have reached agreement to carry out live experiments. The new Prestel Viewdata terminal will have a provision for sensors which can be connected to electricity and gas meters, and make remote meter readings possible: object, manpower saving.

Immediately there is another public outcry. Big Brother, it seems, is not only going to watch you, he is also going to monitor your fuel consumption. Cartoonists resurrect late-seventies fuel conservation advertisements, reading this time: 'Save it — or else'.

As it is 1984, the jokers are out in force. A London party worker writes a paper showing how Prestel Viewdata could be used on polling days to keep track of which supporters have and have not gone to the polls — this would be on a real-time basis based on terminals (in supporters' homes) near all polling booths. Senior party national officials stamp on her, but not before it has become public and led to leaders in *The Times*, and — it being the middle of summer — cries from back-bench Members of Parliament for a recall of the Commons as a matter of national urgency.

Then the idea of Tele-Penitence is resurrected, a tongue-in-cheek joke. This is the proposal for the creation of a Viewdata database listing all possible sins. The would-be penitent subscriber indicates which sins he has committed, how often, and is asked the degree of seriousness ascribed to each one. Viewdata then states the appropriate penance to be carried out, and give absolution. An aged Monsignore is found to give the idea his blessing, and endless television programmes ensue. An Anglican bishop comments that the ecumenical movement having once more come to a halt, perhaps we should consider the use of such systems as Viewdata in the search to bring the Churches together.

Nobody of course has initially noticed that in listing sins with penalties 'attached', it takes little wit to work out which are the most pleasurable, or which of the pleasurable carry the smallest penalty.

But it would not be Britain if everybody missed this, and sure enough, it is pointed out in *The Times* correspondence page. In the midst of the resultant uproar, voices are heard suggesting the possibility of meditation by Viewdata, in which the regularity of the Viewdata flashing character facility could be of assistance. Insert your own mantra. *Time Out* reveals that the bio-feedback proponents have been using the facility for just this sort of purpose during the last three years.

In the background, a voice is quietly heard to suggest that what we need are sacrifices by Viewdata. Correspondence ensues with people asking how this is to be carried out. (A letter not printed by *The Times* from the successors to the Baader Meinhoff 'gang' points out that for the first time the executive classes — not just the capitalists — are using television as a *direct* medium of oppression of the working class. Previously, they write, the executive classes did not use television except indirectly to sell pap to the workers. Now they use it in the quietness of their homes late at night, working out how to further tyrannise the revolutionary masses. 'We have infiltrated the service companies', they write, 'and will use the 3000-volt potential in the receiver so as to execute some of the more notorious offenders.')

It has been an even longer, hotter summer than in 1983. In the Information Provider area, changes are afoot. An experiment (first partially carried out in 1978) in which mail order houses put their agents on line has proved successful, and a major mail order company announces that from next year this will be extended nationwide, with improved agents' commission. The essentials of the system rely on the agent having a bank account, collecting from customers in the usual way, and pumping in orders to the mail order house which then directly debits from the agent's bank account. Reduced administrative costs at the mail order house can then be passed on to the agent in the form of increased commission.

A correspondent in the trade journals points out, originally, that this is the thin end of the wedge and that the mail order houses could bypass the agent and go directly to the customer. A mail order house replies that even with the best of systems as yet, something can go wrong, and that a local human interface with groups of customers is still desirable. The company manages to avoid the issue as to whether it will go directly to the customer, bypassing the agent, and a computer journalist digging around discovers the existence of a project team studying the creation of an on-line complaints system which can override the normal company mechanisms and automatically deal with complaints. These being statistically predictable, the company figures that it can cost this machinery into the saving it will make from going over to Prestel Viewdata. But will it eliminate its agents? 'No comment.'

Post Office announces portable Viewdata using mobile radio links, trials to be carried out next year in the Thames Valley.

Closed user groups developing quite rapidly. Among them a LAMSAC facility in which local authorities swap data on how government guidelines in education and housing are being carried out, an extension of an idea of the seventies which arises from work on tele-conferencing systems.

Post Office celebrates tenth anniversary of first public demonstration of Viewdata, and forgets to invite inventor.

1985

Contrary to public expectations, there are hardly any new Viewdata models this year; the industry is too busy trying to meet public demand. Post Office is known to be carrying out wideband data transmission experiments with its new Viewdata receivers, and the results of the first experiments of Viewdata-linked remote meter reading are released. They are marred by a failure in inter-organisation communications: the system is seen to be an improvement, but in Hammersmith and Bootle the meter readers still called.

The overnight mail facility experiments are a success, but are more expensive than initially expected. They do not reduce the need for internal company delivery systems, and Post Office announces that the service is to be refined so that mail is sent directly to addressee where required. Smart company managing director discovers that arrangements can be made for him to select what mail addressed to which executive he wishes to see, without such executive being aware. Same director also discovers that with some tweaking of the internal system, it is quite possible for him to be made privately aware of all departments' figures before meeting their executives — and that this has its uses!

First MSc from London Polytechnic in Viewdata systems design.

Government plans announced in Commons for change in personal taxation system, and for the long-awaited move towards the US system in which the onus is on the taxpayer to make claims. The new forms will be available either on paper or through Prestel Viewdata, with tax guides available in either version. The Prestel version will eventually allow for a conversation between tax inspector and taxpayer, both being able to view the figures under discussion at same time. The ultimate aim is to proceed to a direct-debit system in which, the taxpayer and the inspector having agreed the figures, the taxpayer's bank will be brought into the link; the taxpayer's account will then be directly debited as if this were a simple EFT transaction. Questions are asked in the House: will the taxpayer be able to pay the figures agreed by using the electronic credit card facility? Government reply that no plans afoot for such a radical change.

A week later, one of the Big Five banks mounts an advertising campaign: pay your taxes on credit, easy repayments over twelve months. Facility only available over Prestel.

Xerox announce their Viewdata-linked range of copiers. The first will take copies directly from either in-house or Prestel Viewdata systems, and various models are available; the smallest offering simple copies on A4. Further up the range is a copier under computer control; it has its own in-built microprocessors, which can be set to search Viewdata by code words and print out relevant frames automatically. A colour version is promised for next year.

The AA put Viewdata into their roadside emergency boxes. The facility guides the user through the details of the problem, asks for make of car, year and other data, and the AA centre then transmits this to the appropriate vehicle — which carries a terminal and printer — by radio link.

Post Office announce a Viewdata-switching facility and the Prestel electronic diary. (The latter was first suggested by Rex Malik in *Data Systems* in 1968.) The switching facility is part of the overnight mail service, and will allow business mail to be sent to an addressee at both business and home addresses where he requires. The diary facility allows anyone to put up their forthcoming meetings, birthday reminders, notes, etc., and the system will flash them on the appropriate day and offer a reminder. It is noticeable that one of the first uses is a rash of birthday greetings, Viewdata making it possible to remember on the actual day and still transmit a message.

Sinclair Electronics announce two-inch-screen portable Viewdata, Viewdata-compatible across Europe, a useful Christmas present for those with 'everything'.

1986

The inflation which has been continuing at 9-10 per cent a year throughout the eighties has caused problems for public transport, not least at the booking offices where it has been necessary to change the automatic machines at least once every nine months.

There are now many fare variants depending on times of day and class of user, as well as numerous special offers. A new class of systems appears in which Viewdata systems are linked to coin boxes, saving the frequent change-over of the old ticket printers. The British Rail variant also displays delays of trains, changes and cancellations, and at slack times displays advertising.

The year brings a new breed of information provider into being. Depending on the availability of intelligent Viewdata terminals and the program facility, the new breed offers simulation, and begins by marketing learn-to-drive and learn-to-fly packages, either via Prestel or on tape cassette. An up-market version mixes Viewdata with a video picture. Naturally this cannot be run via a keyboard, and driving wheel units are available at a premium. The only snag is that public demand is higher than expected and no one can deliver, which makes it the hottest toy of the year.

The Post Office announce a limited home experiment in overnight mail via Prestel. The experiment will be based on two types of area, urban and country, and will be run in London and the Peak District. Correspondence ensues about the country experiment, and the fact that the call of the friendly postman is for some people their only daily human contact. Mail by Viewdata will not be the same.

This sparks off a public debate. It has at long last become apparent to politicians that the electronic era brings back to prominence an old argument concerned with social versus economic cost, one which will not go away because the costs of Viewdata and associated systems bear no comparison to similar — but people-cost — dependent systems. The argument has been going on for over a hundred years in one form or another, indeed ever since the advent of the penny post. Now it is not simply a question of whether costs should be spread over the country, so that areas where the service is economic in fact pay *above* the economic cost to support those where it is uneconomic. The issue is much broader, and is best expressed like this. Viewdata may be economic, fast and reliable. Nevertheless, it is not the mail as we have hitherto understood it. Is there any social value to a system which allows an old lady in Inverness to write to her old school chum in Bournemouth, the handwriting on the perfumed paper being as important as the message itself. If so, what is this value? And how is it expressed?

This sort of argument now dominates the stage. It has taken ten years for the Post Office and the Viewdata industry to arrive at a point where the nature of Viewdata is well understood: to accept that Viewdata is a framework technology, and that accordingly building Viewdata systems no longer requires great imagination or seeming high risk commitments. It is in the nature of framework technologies that the components can be permutated in many ways, and that whether or not they are transformed yet again to fill another public need or want has more to do with the demands of everyday life; than filling in gaps in a company's range of products or devising huge potential markets. It is now more a question of building systems enabling us to cross the road than building systems enabling us to wander around the planets. Viewdata has become user driven.

Summary

This is a good point at which to leave the scenario. For we are now dealing with a period ten years after the initial commitment to Viewdata, and ten years is sufficiently far ahead — indeed, possibly even further ahead — than prudent writers dealing in an area with so many dependencies and second-order effects would wish to go.

However, this is not the only reason. All the events we have described are possible and most are likely, even the reactions to them. Many Viewdata technology systems described in this chapter are already under development. Some are not, but it takes very little wit to see that they could and probably will be devised, and in this time scale.

We leave the scenario too at a natural break point. The reader will have noticed that the further ahead we go in time, the more dominated by social consequences the scenario becomes. This too is in keeping with past experience of the introduction of major technologies into society. The important questions become concerned not so much with how and what with, but with why — with effects. This is the stuff of which serious public debate is made.

It leads us naturally to the third and final chapter of this section, the reason why this book and this section were entitled 'The Viewdata Revolution'.

12 Conclusion

What, you might well ask, can there be left to say at this stage? Are there any other major uses to which Viewdata technology can be put, which we have not so far covered? The answer is 'probably', and when they do arise we shall doubtless look at each other wondering why we did not think of them: they will seem to be so obvious.

Are there then also any insights into the nature of Viewdata-type systems which we have not discussed? Well, yes, there are. This alliance between a professional engineer inventor and a writer on information technology, its effects and consequences, would not have come about if we had not agreed that Viewdata technology went further than a listing of services and the fulfilling of all sorts of market demands hitherto not adequately met by the media technologies which came before Viewdata.

Most of what we have written about Viewdata in these pages has had to do with time. A moment's reflection will show that this is one of the cores of the book; a critical effect of a new media is how it alters the time framework in which information can be handled and received, and thus the time framework in which action is taken or the decision made not to take action. If one wants to be 'high falutin' about it, a new media — once established — alters the spatial relationship between the acquiring of knowledge and the taking of action. And that is the stuff which somewhere along the chain leads to change in operations both at the micro-level — the individual looking for an educational car repair course which will eventually lead him/her to withdraw the vehicle from the formal economic system; he will do it himself, rather than paying a company to do so — and at the macro level — numerous individuals acting accordingly and thus destroying the basis of the car repair industry, leading to a sufficient rise in unemployment to rock the system whatever the system may be.

However, anyone can write simple scenarios of this kind: the thoughts and the scenarios are the stuff of pop sociology and how 'information and society' evening courses are made up — the small change of 'gee whizz' journalism.

As with the cliché, whose boring repetition leads to the attribution of the term 'cliché', truth and newness are not the converse of each other. The essence of the cliché after all is that it is usually an over-familiar restatement of the relationship of cause to effect: do this and that will follow.

We seem to have this sort of situation here. And now we wish to introduce one possible major effect of a national Viewdata-type system in being; the reader may have had some glimmering of this effect prior to reading this sentence, but we have not previously made it explicit.

Information handling

The system fills a long-term need: Viewdata technology in embryo has a natural fit against a problem which has plagued us throughout this century, that of handling — i.e. quickly finding our way around — the mass of information on which our activities depend. This is a problem on which immense sums are spent in all the industrial societies, yet we have found no generally agreed solutions at either macro- or micro-levels.

The problem is that of indexing. At which all stout parties will turn round and say: 'You call that a major problem?' Yet a moment's reflection will in fact show that it is so.

It has now become another cliché that we live in an

information society: that more than 50 per cent of working time (we exclude private time, which would make the percentage much higher) is spent handling information. But what do we mean when we talk of people handling information? They are either working with the information that they have, trying to effect change with it whether it is calculation or movement of some kind, or they are trying to relate it with some other information they either have or wish to obtain.

We can use other micro and macro examples. The doctor assimilating, say, the release of information about a new drug and what it will mean to his patients, does so one at a time as they come to see him; the government's — any society's — health service economist now trying to take the inputs from those individual decisions (for it is a good wonder drug) on the costs of the total national health system, does so well after the event, indeed with present systems he has little control; he has not got the necessary clinical experience, yet those individual decisions may well have upset all forecasts as well as the budgets.

So where does Viewdata technology fit in? We wrote in Chapter 1 about the ten-level hierarchic-tree structure of Viewdata systems, and of the power this gives us to find our way through the information. That power is almost as fundamental as the serial order imposed on the way we work in real life by the fact that the alphabet begins with the letter A and ends with Z.

This too may be a difficult notion to grasp, so let us step back a little.

Encyclopaedia concept

The notion of the world encyclopaedia is now an old one; from the library of Alexandria, to Napoleon's thirty wise men who would be able to answer all questions, to the attempts of H.G. Wells. The last is perhaps more germane to our situation: we need to ask what defeated its realisation. The answer is threefold. Firstly, the inability to keep such an encyclopaedia up to date, because of the continuing additions to knowledge. This was a problem at one level of data collection, but at a higher level it was the problem of media. The media — the printed book — did not have the inherent potential to take and reproduce those additions fast enough to prevent their being outmoded by time. The technology and the time factor inherent in the production and dissemination of the knowledge, to make the world encyclopaedia a practical meaningful reality, could not be reconciled.

Secondly, there was the practical problem of translation of information, whether from a different language or from the language of the specialist into that of the audience. At first sight, one cannot see how Viewdata technology changes that. But first sight as ever is likely to be wrong. Very few of us have the ability to speak, write or otherwise present material so that it transcends the limitations of the media we are using; so that what is spoken, written or pictorially presented can be reproduced directly in a different medium without losing its own force and individual characteristics; so that whether we look at it or listen to it, we can say yes, that's how it is, and it is an exact replica. Most of us have to make a translation of some kind, to tailor material both to media and to audience.

One does not expect mass Viewdata systems to make an immediate change in the practice — indeed, there is no reason why they should do so. However, the hierarchic tree structure properly used does allow different levels of complexity to be handled within the same medium so that, say, at level two (the one past the initial indexes) one has up a child's version of the law of relativity, and at level ten it is treated in its full mathematical complexity.

The ability to recombine within one set of mechanisms and conventions, each frame carrying identifiers for the next one down in order of complexity (or back up to something simpler — which is quite possible); the ability to add cross-references — these could lead to a new set of conventions for handling material at the Viewdata level. Usage and exposure are here expected to work as they have done elsewhere.

But at another level, it must never be forgotten that Viewdata technology is the outcome of developments in related fields, and those fields continue to be so related. In both computing and telecommunications immense effort has been made, and equally immense sums expended, on trying to achieve instant translation, whether of language, or the spoken word into the printed form (or vice versa), or of the complex into the simple, or again vice versa.

Much work has for instance been done on schemes in which a complex entry of information is reduced to its key words, enabling the user to flick through a large number of entries quickly in a search for the item which will bear on the problem to which the answer is sought. It would be unreasonable to expect that this work, coming as it does from related technology, will not impact on the growth of Viewdata technology.

The last two sentences in the above paragraph do in fact bear on our third and final reason why the Wells encyclopaedia came to naught. It has to do with the problem of order, of structure and of establishing relationships, which is what the indexing problem is directly about. What does this piece of information relate to that I do not already know? How does it relate to it? And how do I find out without missing what might otherwise be obvious?

The problem defeated Wells and it has, at least one of us believes, defeated almost all paper media encyclopaedia producers. Again one has to think through why it should have done so. Complexity of information; changing information; inability to relate all information to a common structure capable of handling it, which means exceptions, which in turn means that the chances of missing something increase as the material grows: these are some of the reasons. But the overriding reason needs to be restated: the failure was inherent in the medium.

If such an encyclopaedia can not be made to work effectively within Viewdata, then it will be a failure of commission rather than one of omission. For Viewdata can be seen as a system in which the basic structuring imposed on the information according to amount of detail and place in the subject hierarchy (and that almost without end) makes the realisation of the Wellsian dream practicable — which is not of course to say that it initially makes it likely.

Of course, while this is theoretically possible, the full database would tax the technology currently available, let alone the provision of storage or its cost. (The calculation to make the point can be done quickly: we are talking roughly of one K, or one thousand bytes, a Viewdata frame, or *one hundred million megabyte* on line if we wish for a fast response on all items within the database. This would be equivalent to putting together more than 100 000 of the largest disc drives currently available, for it must be remembered that each disc drive is not entirely full with useable data but also stores its own operating instructions, which can decrease the useful storage by as much as 30 or so per cent. There are of course other ways of handling the storage problem, notably mass storage tape units, but here the access time goes up sharply. Whatever means are chosen, the point that we are making is that the solution to the problem would be complex and very very expensive as the technology on the market exists in the late nineteen seventies.)

It is worth making that point, not because one expects it to be realisable with the present stage of the technology, or even to indicate that it might be worth trying to put this together. Rather, the point is this: one does not have to build the full system to make the basic structure work; level twelve could be reached with surprising little technology within the basic structure, though obviously with some restriction. The point is, however, that one hundred megabyte on line is capable of swallowing immense collections of information.

Thus we have possibilities of putting up in an indexed orderly and rational fashion, say, the entire parliamentary record on one database, and still having the capability within the same system of continuing to add to it daily as far off into the future of society as anyone might care or wish to look.

The case of the Wells encyclopaedia or a modern derivative is the extreme case. We do not suggest that such an enterprise should be undertaken, rather that it *could* now be practically undertaken were the demand for access to that information to be there.

Less ambitious collections of data then really should not be a serious problem. The information, it hardly needs pointing out at this juncture, would be easily accessible, whether you consider accessability to be a problem of indexing or a problem of access at the time required.

In the end the mix of technologies which, brought together, become Viewdata technology help us to solve problems which beset all of us, whether at a trivial or more serious level. This is why such technologies will be more and more widely used.

That knowledge is power is a meaningless statement: the ability to obtain knowledge and utilise it, fundamental to using Viewdata whether you regard it as an information retrieval or a communications system, however, does perhaps help to reduce the information chaos we now live in, and that does give us some power — with a small 'p' — over our environment.

The last word

We do not claim that Viewdata systems are enough: just that they arrive at the right time, a time when related technologies have given us sometimes considerable control over specific areas. National Viewdata systems are going to be the web in which those sit, and could enable us to relate the systems one to another and the systems to ourselves.

This is not going to happen overnight. Yet, when it does, it could well lead to changes in society. We have not gone down the road which states that because such systems exist, therefore we are all going to work at home. We do not in fact believe this. Rather, we prefer to think of Viewdata's relationship to people as being linked to time and how it is used. For there are no social hours to Viewdata systems: they work round the clock, and give access all the time. As the car has changed the majority's relationship to distance, so

Viewdata could change the relationship to information. It becomes like water: on tap.

In the end, though technology is neutral in itself — albeit usually devised to overcome a problem about which someone feels sufficiently deeply to devote time to seeking a solution — Viewdata technology applied on a wide scale is a technology suited to a democracy. True, there are Big Brother overtones — almost any media has them. However, it is a technology which will work best when dealing with complexity for societies which have massive volumes of information and almost as massive numbers of people independently wishing to find their way through it.

One could in fact go further: Viewdata technology is a democratic technology, if such a term can be coined. And it is so whether the democracy is that of the market — people will pay for what they want and what they use — or whether it is of the egalitarian, open-government and open-society, co-operate or else, school.

It should not be necessary to add that it is disliked by some — and they are found on either side of this debate. For it can be expected to upset the traditional order of things. But we comfort ourselves with a thought that could have been uttered at any time during history: that that is what the traditional order of things is there for.

Appendix: And now, Videotex...

As you would expext in a technology which is fast developing — technically, commercially, politically — much has happened since we started to write this book. When we thought of it in early 1978, Viewdata was called simply Viewdata: the name Prestel had not been invented by the UK Post Office. The UK system, though not on its own, was however the only system to which a national telecommunications provider was committed: the rest could genuinely be called experimental.

In the summer of 1979, the situation has been transformed, and enough in Europe for the European Community to become involved. It has taken the view that there are a new class of information/communication systems emerging which could do for text and elementary graphics what the telephone has done for voice.

In June 1979, the Commission called a conference attended by senior telephone authority executives, senior broadcasting organisation executives, representatives of Information Providers, major manufacturers, and senior civil servants from national government ministries who would have to become involved. One of the authors, Rex Malik, was present representing the users of Europe: a lone voice for 220 million people.

The conference had been called to consider the implications

of the new technologies, and to start discussing such questions as: If these systems are a new class, and destined to become a commercial reality, to play an important part in people's lives, then such questions as, when, how, and in what form, are already worth considering.

Additionally, these systems will have potential implications at a European level for manufacturing industry, users both in the home and in business, the overall 'electronic infrastructure', employment, and the needs of the various language groups in Europe. These are of course areas in which the Commission has a responsibility, and thus the occasion for the conference. Should the Community allow the technology to come to fruition independently in each country, or should it play a role? And if so, what sort of role?

The Commission had had studies prepared for the conference to consider. One of the consultant's reports put it like this.

> Videotex is of the greatest importance as a catalytic concept at the junction of the converging telecommunications, computer, broadcasting and publishing industries, and it will lead to:
>
> - Mass domestic market for electronic systems and services
> - Mass electronic publishing
> - Acceleration of key standards and regulatory development

But what is all this about 'Videotex'? The Commission found itself facing a host of developments, and a host of differing names and terminologies. After consultation, it came up with the following schema to encompass them all, at least all the EEC developments. The list is given below.

General

Videotex

A communication system in which digitally encoded frames are transmitted for reception by a modified TV set where a limited number of frames are stored and displayed. Most systems have a colour capability employing the fundamentals red, green, blue (on or off) in any combination thereby giving 8 colours (black, white, red, green, yellow, blue, magenta, cyan).

Broadcast Videotex

The generic name for Videotex systems employing one way communication. The entire set of frames is transmitted repeatedly, the user specifies and the receiver selects, stores and displays the required information. Most systems at present are inserting the information in the interframe blanking of a TV signal transmitted over the air.

Interactive Videotex

The generic name for Videotex systems employing two way communication. The user is able to communicate with the system to specify his requirements. Single frames are transmitted to the receiver, where they are stored and displayed. Most systems at present are using the public telephone network with a modem (modulator demodulator) at a speed of 1200 bit/s from the system to the receiver and at 75 bit/s from the receiver to the system (1200/75 bit/s).

Note: These expressions are not the ones used currently within CCITT (Comité Consultatif International de Télégraphique et Téléphonique) but it is likely that they might be used by this committee in the future.

Appendix 173

Existing Videotex Systems

Teletext

The UK system for the broadcast Videotex agreed by the BBC (British Broadcasting Corporation), IBA (Independent Broadcasting Authority) and BREMA (British Radio Equipment Manufacturers Association).

Viewdata

The system of the UK developed by the UK Post Office Telecommunications Department for the interactive Videotex.

Antiope

Antiope is the Videotex system (both the broadcast and the interactive) for France which is developed by the CCETT (Centre Commun d'Etudes de Télévision et de Télécommunication) in Rennes.

Telidon

This is the Canadian proposal for an interactive Videotex system.

Videotex Services (operational or planned)

Ceefax

The broadcast Videotex service offered in the UK by the BBC using the Teletext system.

Oracle

The broadcast Videotex service offered in the UK by IBA using the Teletext system.

Prestel

Prestel is the public interactive Videotex service offered by the UK Post Office since early April this year using the Viewdata system.

Télétel

The experimental interactive Videotex service of France offered by the French PTT in a field trial in Velizy (a suburb of Paris) using the Antiope system.

Bildschirmtext

The experimental German service of interactive Videotex which uses at present the Viewdata system, the character generator of which will be adapted for special German needs (e.g. ä, ö, ü, ...) for the field trial to be done around Dusseldorf.

But what is it that the Commission seeks? The answer can be put quite simply and tersely. That Videotex develops as rapidly as possible, and as compatibly as possible across Europe, without upsetting the pace at which development is proceeding. It seeks for European standards, but it is wise enough to understand that were it to try to have agreement on standards come about too early, it might in fact slow down the pace of a technology which is being developed faster in Europe than anywhere else. Standardisation should come from interfacing arrangements between the various countries which do not cut across the pace of development: a difficult exercise and one which is just beginning.

If one concentrates on interactive Videotex systems, there are four major countries currently involved: two in the Community — the UK and France — and two outside: Japan and the United States. There are also minor developments elsewhere, of which the Canadian experiment, Telidon, is probably the most interesting and important, though it relates much more to computing and graphics than to the mass market.

Appendix 175

This book has been primarily about the technology being developed in the UK, the country currently in the lead and the first to mount a public service. That service began in London in the spring of 1979, and will be going partly national in the autumn of 1979, around the time this book first appears.

It has already been beset by problems, as we indicated could happen. The set manufacturers have not committed as much as either they or the Post Office expected by this time: there are controversies about who is to blame, with the set manufacturers claiming that it is the fault of the integrated circuit chip manufacturers — the manufacturers of the modem and decoder — and the chip manufacturers saying in private that it is the fault of the set manufacturers, not being prepared to order in large enough quantities and asking for unrealistic prices. And everybody blames the Post Office for unrealistically high charges. This is normal and not unexpected. The facts are that as of today, no real user has as yet paid the economic price for the use of the service: the bills are still to come.

The Post Office has indicated that it may well go down the route of purchasing Viewdata units, units which could be separately added to a television receiver, and sold to existing television users to enable them to receive and use Prestel. The current talk on the market is of the price being initially £100, though £50 is thought to be more realistic if these units were to be manufactured and sold in any quantity. However, they should be thought of as no more than a temporary expedient. Manufacturers with whom one of the authors has talked have privately indicated that a production line for fully integrated Prestel-Viewdata colour receivers could run on volumes of around 80 000 or so sets a year, and that at these volumes the sets would come on the market at a premium above existing colour television receivers of between £100 and £200, at present price levels.

The Post Office is meanwhile forecasting that though production is slow to start up, nevertheless it soon expects to see more Prestel subscribers than it currently has Telex subscribers, though there are nearly 80 000 Telex terminals installed.

Meanwhile Teletext continues to grow, albeit slowly. There are approximately 20 000 sets equipped to receive the BBC and Independent Television services now in use.

When you turn to the UK's main European competitor, France, the situation is more complex. The French have been driven by different considerations to those which have driven the British. Where the British began by asking how we could make better use of the communications capability we already have, to make more use of the telephone network, the French began by creating a highly sophisticated packet-switching network, and then asking themselves what could be slung around it — apart from the equally sophisticated users, mainly technically inclined, who were to be its prime users.

The generic name for all the services in France is ANTIOPE. The receiver differs in one key essential in that instead of entering the receiver's electronics via the aerial socket, ANTIOPE enters via an electronic interface, which in the long term must give more flexibility.

Broadcast or Teletext ANTIOPE currently offers two limited services. First, there is ANTIOPE-Bourse, a broadcast service giving stock market information which is offered in Paris and Lyon; secondly, there is ANTIOPE Meteo, a weather information service aimed at professionals; the building trade, agriculture, energy industry, transportation. Both services came on the air early in 1978, though the users as yet are few in number.

Interactive ANTIOPE or Teletel will start its public trials with a 3000 set experiment in the suburbs of Paris; Velizy, Versailles, Jouy-en-Josas, in 1980. It will offer data on medical services such as which chemists are open and when, hospital services, trains and airline timetables, offers of employment, news, stock exchange data, product information, legal and economic information, and a limited message service.

Clearly, France is committed to its services at a senior government level. This has become quite apparent as a result

Appendix 177

of moves made by French administration to knock heads together and have the television manufacturers agree a standard and further agree that from late 1980, no television set will be built in France which does not have the agreed ANTIOPE interface, so that, willy-nilly all sets of French manufacture purchased in France from 1981 onwards will have an ANTIOPE capability, even if additional units have to be purchased to make it work.

However probably the most dramatic move has come from the French PTT. The French telephone service, long the joke of Europe (it used to be said that half of France was waiting for a phone, while the other half was waiting for a dialling tone) is being rapidly modernised, and extended to give a truly national service. However such a service would also require, if handled conventionally, the production of immense numbers of phone directories. Everywhere else these are printed volumes, using paper, which then needs to be distributed. It means in turn that few people ever have really current directories, which means in turn massive directory enquiry facilities have to be provided. What the French have identified is that the costs of distribution are such that another service could be provided using Videotex technology, and that this could be run on the marginal difference — it is a large margin — between the two.

In 1981 the French PTT intend to instal between 200,000 and 250,000 small black and white videotex terminals with telephone subscribers. They will be integral with the telephone handset, and come with it under the normal rental: there is no extra charge. The target cost of these terminals, said to be obtainable by some manufacturers, is around £35: French Francs 300. These terminals will then be used by subscribers to access a computerised telephone directory system. It is obvious that the same terminal could also be used to work with other ANTIOPE type services, and the French PTT are well aware of this.

They stated at the Commission's conference that it was their intention to have 10 million subscribers on line to this system by 1985, and that by 1992 there would be 30 million subscribers, by which time they would be well on the way to putting all subscribers up. What we are witnessing then is an attempt to create the world's first truly on-line society.

By contrast, Japan, which has the longest history of experimentation with television systems to discover additional uses, has as yet no plans to go beyond experimental services. The Japanese aproach has been substantially different to that of the European. They began in the late sixties, at the time of the euphoria for cable television, and they started by trying to create a master plan, 'The Information Society 2000', into which such systems could fit.

The purposes of the ministries involved may be social, the purposes of the industries involved are economic. They talk of social systems using leading edge technologies, and begin by considering the creation of such systems as MPIS, a Multi-Purpose Information System for rural areas, and AMPS, an Air Pollution Monitoring and Control System.

However, if one is considering analogues to Videotex, one begins elsewhere. Five systems need to be considered. First is the experiment to mount a broadcast Videotex service, CIBS (Character Information Broadcasting System), which was run last year, based on work done over five years, and which is eventually expected to become a public service. This too concentrates on such data as weather and news.

CIBS is however really out of the mainstream of Japanese developments. The first in this stream, and by far the best known outside has been the Tama New Town project, a CCIS system (or Coaxial Cable Information System). This provides a number of television services over cable, retransmission, original broadcast, broadcast and response from individual households, still picture transmission on demand from a keyboard attached to receiver, and two types of facsimile transmission, one for an 'electronic newspaper', the other for memo type information. There were also some control facilities provided using the same cable: water meter reading, disaster (fire) prevention sensors which were added to some sets after the conclusion of the main experiment in late 1977. The experiment covered some 500 households, not all of which however had all the facilities involved. The major purpose of the Tama New Town experiment, as Japanese officials tell you, was to find a way to provide a commercial service using coaxial cable.

HI-OVIS (Higashi Ikoma Optical Visual Information System) installed in a suburb of Osaka, and which had early in 1979 cost $25 million so far, arose out of internal Japanese competition. It was developed under the aegis of MITI, the umbrella technical cooperation Japanese Ministry, with a firm eye on international trade. This is an experiment to exploit two-way cable possibilities, using fibre optics cables, which goes further than the original CCIS experiment. People can not only receive a TV image, they can also transmit one. The system can also handle facsimile, it enables the user to call up information stored in a microfiche facility at the CCIS centre, and can be used by the subscriber to access such data as local weather, utility breakdowns, on-duty doctors in the area, and traffic information. It is Tama New Town all over again, but using more advanced technology, and providing more facilities.

HI-OVIS though still in use has been followed by an experimental system, whose trials with 1500 sets installed begins in late 1979, called CAPTAINS, or Character and Pattern Telephone Access Information Network System. CAPTAINS begins to resemble Prestel-Viewdata, but there are some important differences. Among them is the special provision that the Japanese have had to make due to the peculiarities of the written Japanese language.

In written Japanese, one uses Kanji characters, which are Chinese ideographs, and Hiragana characters, Japanese consonant and vowel combinations, which to the foreigner look somewhat similar. Then there are the Katakana terms, words taken from foreign languages, and Roman numerals.

CAPTAINS uses 2965 Kanji/Hiragana characters, plus 64 Katakana, plus 96 alphanumeric characters — not all of which are numbers but come into the numerals set.

It is possible to restrict the storage requirement by the

careful selection of a vocabulary which does not require much storage; however, we can get some idea of the storage requirement from a Japanese calculation with DAVINS (see below) that it needs roughly 300 bits to store a Kanji character. Were one wishing to store the full Japanese industrial standard of 6349 characters, we could be writing of sets requiring around 256K bytes. Even with the restricted 'alphabet' with which CAPTAINS starts — 480 Kanji characters, 480 small Kana characters, and 480 small roman characters: a mixutre of Kanji, Kana, and Roman, 1080 in all — the local storage requirement would be heavy, and when CAPTAINS was conceived it was thought to be too expensive.

Hence the need for a centrally driven system in which the character generator is not with the user but the computer centre. There is of course a penalty to be paid. For the experimental period, the CAPTAINS' centre is separated from the database centre. The user requests information through commands from the keypad, the centre calls up the data from the database centre, transforms the data retrieved into video patterns and transmits it to the terminal. This is its weak spot. The time taken to accede to a request may be anywhere between 15 and 30 seconds a frame. But, say senior Japanese researchers, the Japanese are not that patient.

Nevertheless, the Japanese are treating CAPTAINS as a serious experiment, and not only in terms of technological development. The Ministry, taking a leaf out of the UK Post Office book, has organised an association of Information Providers which includes 20 newspaper companies, 23 advertising agencies, 24 publishers, 11 tourist agencies, 19 department stores, and 19 broadcasting organisations and public utilities. They will provide the information for the 1500-set experiment, and expect to continue when CAPTAINS or its successor become a full fledged public service.

The information available includes shopping data, educational material, hobbies, public information both administrative and social, and news — general, professional, and foreign language. One has the impression that one of the first markets envisaged for CAPTAINS is the foreign tourist market, and that among the first users will be the hotels catering to foreign visitors to Japan.

CAPTAINS is obviously not the answer. Currently the thinking is that the answer would be a system like Viewdata which had the facilities of CCIS and HI-OVIS. A Viewdata-type system is now under development by Fujitsu. It is called DAVINS (Data and Video Information Network System). It is being developed by Fujitsu, in cooperation with CAPTAINS, and with a MITI contribution towards the development costs. Here, the character generator is in the local set, thus providing the speed of response that CAPTAINS lacks.

When one turns to the US, one is faced with a totally different situation: there is as yet no American Videotex/Viewdata equivalent, though INSAC Data Systems, the British software export subsidiary of Britain's National Enterprise Board has taken a licence from the UK Post Office and has sold British Viewdata technology to GT & E, America's second largest telecommunications corporation. The sale has only recently been concluded and no details of any proposed services are as yet available. And the French PTT have concluded an agreement with that major broadcasting organisation CBS whereby CBS will mount an experiment in Saint Louis, Missouri using the ANTIOPE standard.

American developments have in the past followed a route more analogous to that of the Japanese, concentrating on the use that could be made of cable television system, and most of the American experiments, of which there have been many, have followed this path, though so far without much more than local success. Perhaps the best known of these systems in Warner's QUBE in Cleveland in many ways similar to HI-OVIS, which in its mix of offerings gives a remote voting facility.

The reasons for America's slowness have much to do with its legislative climate, and the separation enforced on computing and communications, a separation much weakened in the last couple of years, but which was previously thought to be a major obstacle. And of course, America just did not see the possibilities in time, as we noted earlier.

However, there are some American broadcast videotex services, notably Info-text by Micro-TV in Philadelphia, and Teledata, by KSL TV in Saltlake City, both of which look remarkably like UK Teletext services. There is also a Public Broadcasting Service out of Washington, using an ABC developed system which makes it easier for the deaf to watch television. (This service is similar to the route being pursued by the BBC in the UK, which hopes eventually to start a captioning service for its television broadcasting, a standard system for the deaf.)

Perhaps the most interesting US proposal is the 'Green Thumb' proposal from the US Department of Commerce's National Weather Service and the US Department of Agriculture for a service aimed primarily at farmers, which is to start its trials this year, and to be run as a full service from 1981. Green Thumb's service will be accessible via a standard television and special interface boxes. These boxes will include a modem, microprocessor and storage, as well as the keypad to provide access.

The user will call up data, which will then be dumped into his local store, over the telephone system, after which the line will be disconnected and the data can be accessed locally on an off line basis. The data will include weather at a detailed and local level, agricultural information which one can consider educational, and market price data. There are also expected to be some facilities which are not so easily classifiable, including extensions of the standard rural party line phone system allowing 'meetings' to take place without anyone having to move.

Green Thumb is an interesting experiment in that it is said there are some two million possible installations in America, if one just restricts it to the agricultural community, and the nexus is primarily economic. It can be considered possibly as the largest 'closed user group' so far identified by anyone.

It is a good place to end, for since the bulk of this book was written, an argument has been raging in Videotex circles. Which will fly first: Public Service Videotex, or Private Service

Videotex, Videotex aimed at the professionals and the business community. If it is the first, then mass market economics are all important. If it is the second, then they lose that importance, the costs can be related much more closely to those which existing computer service users expect to pay. It is an argument to which of course there is as yet no answer: the data on which to base a conclusion will not arrive anywhere till 1980-1. However, that there can be such an argument at this stage indicates that everybody expects that Videotex/Viewdata/ CAPTAINS/Telidon/The Federal Republic of Germany's Bildschirmtext version of Viewdata/Green Thumb and the rest are here to stay.

Index

ANTIOPE, 29, 173, 176
AT&T, 11, 25, 56

Babbage, Charles, 107
Baran, Paul, 11
Birmingham, 43-4, 54
Benelux, 21
British Airways, 90
Bildschirmtext, 174

Cashless Society, 9, 11, 81, 83-4
CEEFAX, 173
Characters, 15, 51, 67-8
Characteristics, 15
Chess, 108-111
Closed User Groups, 121, 123-5, 145
Colour, 8, 127
Compatability, 8, 21, 29
Computing, 6, 82
Computers, 51, 54, 62, 68, 78-9, 83, 91, 108, 111
Credit Cards, 91-2

Data, digital nature of, 18, 133
  search, 37-8
  structure, 12-14, 38
    hierarchic tree, 13-14, 37, 164, 165
Davies, Donald, 106

Economics, 32, 48, 71, 119-120, 137-43, 148, 160
Education, Computer Aided Instruction (CAI), 98-102
  Computer Aided Learning (CAL), 98-102
Electronic Mail, 10, 48, 80, 159
Encyclopaedia, 164-8
European Economic Community, 171

Fedida, Sam, 1
French, the, 21, 173, 176-7
Frame, 15, 65
Future of Broadband Communications, 10

Future of the Telephone Industry, 11

Greenberger, Martin, 9
Green Thumb, 182
Guinness Book of Records, 26

Indexing, 119, 163, 166
Information providers, 24, 123, 155-6
INSAC, 30
ITT, 29

Jaguar XJ, 35-8, 40
Japan, CCIS, 179
   CIBS, 179
   CAPTAINS, 179-80
   DAVINS, 180-1
   HI-OVIS, 179

London, 43-4, 54, 150, 154, 159

Malik, Rex, 158, 170
Market, Mass, 6-7, 20, 21, 58
Maze game, 108-9
Medium, a new, 1, 6
Messages, 58-65
Message services, 59-65, 73-79, 113, 117, 146-8, 150
Microprocessor, 23, 69, 105-107, 111, 147
Modem, 18-19
MOO, 108

Network, phone, 18
Network, technology, 50-59
Norwich, 43-4, 54

ORACLE, 173

Packet switching, 56, 58, 111, 118, 148
Parkhill, Douglas, 9
Pask, Gordon, 100
Post Office, 2-4
   telecommunications provider, 2, 17, 30
   as publisher, 3, 24
   Prestel, 2-5, 59-63, 103, 105, 116, 131-4, 144-159, 174
Printer, 51, 66-8, 145
Principles, 13
Prompt, 60
Protocols, 12, 16

QUBE, Warner's, 181

Recorder, audio cassette, 65-6, 151, 159-60

Simplicity of system, 13, 15
Simulation, 101
Skills, lack of requirement for, 7
Software, 11, 16
Stock Exchange, 126
Storage, 51
Switching, digital, 17

Telephone, 3, 17, 62-3, 76-7
Telesoftware, 105-6
Teletext, 2, 8, 21, 29, 112, 153
Teletel, 173, 176
Telex, 50, 72-3, 147
Telidon, 173-4
Turing, Alan, 107-9

United Kingdom, 17

United States, 10, 20, 21, 84-5

Videotex, 171-2, 174
Voice, 19
Visual Display Terminal, 20

West Germany, 174
Whitbread, 126-7